WARDEN FORCE
Worst of the Worst
And Other True Game Warden Adventures

by Terry Hodges

REVIEWS FOR THE *WARDEN FORCE* SERIES

"The entire Warden Force series is a testament to the dedicated, hard-working game wardens not only in California but across the nation. Most people never see these men and women or even consider them. But they put their lives on the line every day to protect and preserve our natural resources. The "Warden Force" books are well written and highly entertaining. If you enjoy true adventures, humor, and the outdoors you will certainly enjoy these books."

~ Ron

***

"Terry Hodges has received national and state writing awards. Having read this book, I can certainly understand why. He is definitely a gifted and talented writer and storyteller. If you enjoy reading about the outdoors, wildlife or law enforcement, this book and probably the whole series should be at the top of your must-read list. Well done, Terry Hodges! I would give this book 10 stars if Amazon would let me."

~ William McPeck

"I always look for the "surprise" in a book that makes it great. Terry Hodges understands how to use surprise as an element of a good story and getting to wisdom. The preface points out three surprises often drawn from Hodges' game warden accounts: "California has more natural diversity of wildlife and wildlife habitat than any other state"—and many of its own citizens do not yet realize that this is a rural state; it is not mainly urban. And some of the most depraved crimes are committed in the rural areas—it is not our urban centers which are the "high crime" areas.

A second misconception which covers a surprise is that game wardens and conservation officers "are at greater risk of being assaulted and killed in the line of duty" than almost any other profession. Whatever else we think of the predators and abusers among us, this book documents the fact that we also harbor and pay great heroes who protect our most precious assets.

These stories enable us to stand beside our heroes who protect our habitats. Our heroes still exist. We join in appreciating them and for doing what they do—combatting the high crimes against Nature committed by some very ignorant, depraved, and well-armed human beings. Our wardens are heroes. Readers can join those who have received, and will receive, California's highest honor, the Medal of Valor."

~ Tom Key

"This is a great collection of stories. As an avid outdoorsman, I enjoy reading these as they are relatable to anyone that enjoys hunting and/or fishing. Each story gives enough detail so that you don't feel like something is missing but not so much that it becomes tiresome and drawn out. The length of each story seems to be just right for people like myself (kids, full time job, weekend warrior) who are busy, yet love to read engaging stories."

~ Michael Shaffer

***

"Hodges is a gifted writer able to let you imagine you are right there experiencing the workings of California's game wardens. I have read most of his books and thoroughly enjoy his writing. He is able to capture factual events mixed with creativity to describe events in a manner that puts you there. Anyone who enjoys the outdoors will appreciate this book."

~ John Johnson

***

"Just when you think that something more bizarre can't occur, the next story doesn't disappoint with another amazing tale of wildlife law enforcement escapades."

~ Kent

"I'm not a hunter, hiker, or a fisherman. I'm a life-long city kid, but I'm hooked. I love the underlying simplicity of identifiable good guys and bad guys, but what really hooked me is the author's ability to make me feel like I'm in the middle of situations I never even nearly experienced. I find myself wondering with the game wardens over how to set a trap for the bad guys and then eagerly reading the ensuing action, sharing the anticipation of success. Many of the stories end with an unanticipated twist, always resulting in a smile of satisfaction. Can't beat these stories for easy reading, education, suspense, and enjoyment."

~ Amazon Reviewer

***

We have every one of Terry's books save this one. Can't wait for it to arrive. Terry has developed a mastery in storytelling. You are there. When he discusses being out in the middle of the night, I feel like reading under the blanket with a flashlight. Truly. The easy read is perfection as well as understandable, but have to force myself to put it down as I don't want it to end so quickly. You'll better understand what wardens have to do other than check fishing licenses."

~ Bill Adelman

WARDEN FORCE
THE WORST OF THE WORST
and Other True Game Warden Adventures

TERRY HODGES
California Department of Fish and Game, Retired

Season 9: Episodes 101-114

Warden Force: The Worst of the Worst and Other True Game Warden Adventures (Season 9 - Episodes 101-114)

ISBN: 978-1629672175 (Paperback)
Library of Congress Control Number: 2021917352

Copyright ©2021 Terry Hodges

www.GameWarden.net
www.WardenForce.com

All rights reserved. No part of this book may be reproduced in any form or by any electronic or mechanical means, including information storage and retrieval systems, without written permission from the author, except in the case of a reviewer, who may quote brief passages embodied in critical articles or in a review.

Trademarked names appear throughout this book. Rather than use a trademark symbol with every occurrence of a trademarked name, names are used in an editorial fashion, with no intention of infringement of the respective owner's trademark.

The information in this book is distributed on an "as is" basis, without warranty. Although every precaution has been taken in the preparation of this work, neither the author nor the publisher shall have any liability to any person or entity with respect to any loss or damage caused or alleged to be caused directly or indirectly by the information contained in this book.

Produced by Brian Schwartz for Wise Media Group.

v9.1

Acknowledgements

To photographer Doug Foglesong for providing the wonderful photograph of a California black bear you see on the cover of this title.

To cover designer Tatiana Villa for her artistic eye and endless revisions.

To audiobook narrator Patrick J. Hinchliffe who worked tirelessly to bring these stories to life.

To publishing consultant Brian Schwartz for his enthusiasm, abundance of creative ideas and expert guidance.

To Joe Graziano, former CFO of APPLE INC., whose friendship has made a great difference in my life.

To Barbara Leitner, who edited the stories in this book. Barbara has been my friend and unpaid editor for years. I've even tried to pay her a time or two. Her response?
"You couldn't afford me."

And finally, to all the readers who have taken time to post a review or drop me a note of appreciation.

Terry Hodges

NOTE TO READER

The stories in this book are true, presented with as much accuracy as memory and existing records permit. I have, however, changed many of the names to protect the privacy of those who have already paid the price for their misdeeds.

Terry Hodges

***

The last three stories (*Death on Snake Mountain, Confession, Heartless Bastard*) first appeared in the magazine, **INTERNATIONAL GAME WARDEN**.
These rare, first-person accounts of events were experienced by the author himself.

To Sandy

Contents

Preface 1
Not Bad for a Fish Cop 3
Fuzz Face, Snake Eyes and Fu Manchu 15
Repeat Offenders 27
Swift Justice 37
The Worst of The Worst 51
Masters of Deception 65
Trouble in Hog Heaven 79
The Cycle 95
The Caviar Connection 105
The Old Pro 121
Zero Choice 131
Death on Snake Mountain 143
Confession 149
Heartless Bastard 155
About the Author 163
The *Warden Force* Series 165

Preface

It surprises many who read my stories to learn of the great diversity of challenges faced by California's Fish and Game wardens. This is probably due to the general misconception of many as to the true nature of this state, the perception that California is mainly urban when in fact the reverse is true. In truth, California has more natural diversity of wildlife and wildlife habitat than any other state and is second only to Alaska in its vast expanses of wilderness.

Readers are also surprised to discover how hazardous my profession can be. Out of necessity, wardens work alone much of the time, often at night, with absolutely no hope for timely backup should things go wrong. And things go wrong, somewhere in the state, with distressing regularity. The dangers of this work are best illustrated by rather grim FBI statistics which clearly show that game wardens and conservation officers in this country are at greater risk of being assaulted or killed in the line of duty than are most sheriff's deputies and police officers.

I mention these facts because I have become increasingly aware of the responsibility that accompanies my telling the stories of California's wardens. It's important to me to tell these stories accurately and to enlighten my readers as best I can as to what it really means to wear a badge and a gun in this state on behalf of wildlife.

With this in mind, I present the following true stories, the experiences of good wardens pursuing a highly challenging and dangerous profession.

Not Bad for a Fish Cop

An old pickup truck crept through the night, its lights out. The driver, Sidney Bogman, a petty criminal, squinted into the darkness ahead to keep the vehicle on a narrow gravel road. It led to the back fence of the Feather River Hatchery, a sprawling riverside facility on both sides of Table Mountain Boulevard, a major public road. In this hatchery, California Department of Fish and Game personnel raised salmon and steelhead trout. Bogman had worked there three years earlier before he was fired.

The back road to the hatchery followed the north bank of the Feather River through undeveloped, willow-studded lowland. Just across the river to the south lay the old city of Oroville, founded 150 years earlier by gold miners. The town's night lights provided just enough glow for Bogman to see to drive.

Upon arriving at a seldom-used gate in the six-foot chain link fence surrounding the hatchery, Bogman stopped and stepped out. From the bed of his pickup, he withdrew a crowbar and a hammer. A chain fastened with a stout padlock secured the gate. Bogman slipped one end of the crowbar through the hasp of the padlock. With the hammer, he struck the bar a sharp blow next to the padlock. Something in the padlock fractured, and the lock fell open. Bogman opened the gate, slipped back behind the wheel and drove inside.

After passing through an open storage yard of old equipment, he stopped at a gasoline pump near the hatchery's water treatment building. He stepped out with a flashlight and warily looked around. He then approached the door, withdrew a large folding knife from his pocket, and with the opened blade he expertly slipped back the bolt on the door lock.

Stepping inside the building, he snapped on a light and approached an electrical control panel. He briefly studied a row of switches and snapped on the one labeled "Gas Pump." He then hurried outside to the gasoline pump and began pumping gas into the near-empty fuel tank of his pickup truck.

In the back of Bogman's pickup were two empty 55-gallon drums. When the pickup's tank was full, he hauled the hose and gas nozzle up into the pickup's bed and began filling the drums. It was slow going, and Bogman glanced often toward the front of the hatchery, the direction from which danger would approach.

At the time, the California State Police held jurisdiction over state facilities. But it was not so much them who worried him. They would occasionally drive through the hatchery complex and shine their spotlights around. But the far greater danger was that posed by the Fish and Game wardens who prowled the river adjacent to the hatchery at all hours of the day and night in search of salmon poachers. Also, the wardens often used the hatchery's large walk-in refrigerator and freezer for evidence storage, and it was a common occurrence for wardens to appear in the middle of the night to store poacher-killed deer or other illegally taken game.

But on this night, Bogman was lucky. He finished pumping gas, turned off the switch to the gas pump and relocked the door to the building. When he drove out the back of the hatchery grounds, he closed the gate behind him, wrapped the chain around it and put the broken lock back in place such that the gate appeared to be locked. Only then did Bogman leave the area, successful in his petty crime against the former employers who had cheerfully dumped him.

A few days later, a hatchery employee performed the weekly ritual of "sticking" the hatchery's 500-gallon gas tank. This meant inserting a calibrated wooden dip stick into the gas tank to determine the amount of fuel remaining within. This figure would be compared with gas logs maintained for the various State vehicles that were fueled from the tank. The total fuel pumped into the State vehicles plus the fuel remaining in the tank would roughly add up to 500 gallons. But on this day, there was a problem. Over 100 gallons of fuel were missing from the tank.

The employee reported the missing fuel to the hatchery manager, who immediately reported the matter to the state police. Their local office was actually on the hatchery grounds, on the opposite side of Table Mountain Boulevard from the water treatment building. The gas theft had occurred within a quarter mile of the state police office.

Six weeks passed, and then it happened again. Hatchery employees found well over 100 gallons of fuel missing from their big gas tank. Was it an inside job? The hatchery manager briefly considered this question, but he was certain that none of his employees were gas thieves. He again informed state police of the theft. In response, the state police promised to increase their drive-throughs of the hatchery grounds. But the fuel thefts continued. As months passed, gas continued to disappear from the storage tank every few weeks.

It was about this time that Lt. James Halber got wind of the problem. Halber supervised the Fish and Game wardens in the area, and he actually lived within a mile of the hatchery. There was something about the hatchery gas thefts that annoyed Halber. It was as though someone was stealing from his family. He took it personally. He therefore decided to take on the task of catching the hatchery's gas bandit.

He first went to the hatchery and studied the scene of the gas thefts. A hatchery employee showed him the gas pump and the switch inside the water treatment building that activated the pump. Halber then walked through the equipment storage area behind the building and spotted the gate. Upon examining the gate, he soon discovered the broken lock which appeared to be securing the locking chain. Aware now how the gas bandit was entering the hatchery, he set about a plan to put him out of business.

Because the thefts were occurring so infrequently, it was a difficult problem to attack. But Halber noted that the average interval between thefts was about five weeks, so he was able to roughly predict a time window when the gas bandit would most likely strike again. When that window began, Halber was there.

On the first night of the likely time window, Halber stashed his patrol vehicle and walked to a hillside overlooking the back part of the hatchery. From there he had a clear view of the water treatment building and the gas pump. There he waited and watched until dawn the following morning. Absolutely nothing happened during the night, not even a drive-through by the state police.

The following night, Halber did it again, and again nothing happened. For three long weary nights he watched the hatchery all night, and the gas bandit didn't show. On the third night, Halber decided that there had to be a better way. He simply couldn't justify the time he was spending keeping the hatchery under surveillance. Then he had an idea.

After managing a few hours of sleep the following morning, Halber phoned the California State Department of Justice, DOJ, in Sacramento. The DOJ maintained a supply of special equipment that was available for temporary use by all law enforcement agencies. Halber had borrowed equipment from them in the past, such as gyro-stabilized binoculars for use in aircraft, "wires" for use in undercover operations, and other problem-solving gizmos.

Upon reaching one of DOJ's gizmo guys, Halber explained his problem.

"I need to monitor a gate," he said. "I need something that will alert me when the gate is opened."

The gizmo guy thought for a moment.

"I think I've got what you need," he said. "Come on down and I'll show it to you."

Two hours later, Halber was there, and the gizmo guy showed him a tiny, battery-operated transmitter linked to a "trip box" by 20 feet of fine, camo-colored wire. Protruding from the trip box was a tiny pin with an eye on one end.

"When this pin is pulled from this box, the transmitter is activated," said the gizmo guy.

He then held up a receiver unit with an antenna on top.

"The transmitter sends out a signal that activates an alarm on this receiver."

He then turned on the receiver, pulled the pin from the trip box, and the receiver began emitting a loud beep.

"But the range is limited, essentially to line of sight."

This presented a problem for Halber, for his house was probably too far away. Then he thought of the Oroville Police Station, which at that time was almost immediately across the Feather River from the hatchery. Problem solved.

"One more thing," said Halber, as he was preparing to leave. "I need a black light kit."

The gizmo guy left the room briefly and returned with a plastic case. He opened the case, revealing what looked like a small fluorescent tube in a fixture. He then held up two small jars.

"Will two colors be enough?" This was in reference to black-light-sensitive paste, which came in different colors. Anything coming in contact with this paste would glow brightly under black light.

"Two would be fine," said Halber. He then thanked the gizmo guy, gathered up his borrowed equipment and went on his way.

Later that afternoon, Halber revisited the rear gate of the hatchery. First, he tied a three-foot length of monofilament fishing line to the pin in the trip box, and he mounted the trip box to the base of the gate post, below the gate's bottom hinge. He concealed the box with rocks and bits of shrubbery. He then ran the camo-colored wire to the transmitter, which he mounted to a fence post and concealed about 15 feet from the trip box. Now he ran the fishing line, securing it to the bottom of the gate such that when the gate was opened, the fishing line would pull the pin out of the trip box.

Halber next went to the water treatment building. He went inside and approached the switch panel. He carried with him the two bottles of black-light-sensitive paste. Dipping his finger into the bottle marked "Red," he smeared the paste on the switch for the gas pump. He then walked outside and closed the door. He now dipped a different finger into the bottle marked "Green" and smeared a fine coating of it on the outside doorknob. The paste was petroleum jelly-based and was all but invisible on the knob. Anyone opening the door or flipping on the gas pump switch would get the paste on their hands.

With his trap now in place, Halber delivered the receiver unit across the river to the police station, explaining to the chief of police and the on-duty dispatcher its purpose. Because Halber personally knew all of the dispatchers and all of the police officers, there was no problem. The Oroville Police Department, or OPD, was firmly behind his plan to bring to an end the misdeeds of the hatchery gas bandit.

When the receiver was plugged in and activated at the OPD dispatcher's table, Halber returned to the gate to test the system.

He removed the broken lock, unwrapped the chain and opened the gate. Immediately he got a radio call from the OPD dispatcher.

"Your gizmo's beeping."

Following the successful test, Halber reset his trap, closing the gate, wrapping the chain and hooking the broken padlock in place. Satisfied with his work, he now left the hatchery and turned his attention to other things. Days passed, then weeks. As time went by, Halber thought less and less about his trap and the gas bandit. But he returned to the hatchery every few days to replenish the black-light paste.

It was about three weeks after Halber had set his trap at the hatchery that he had a chance to return the favor to the Oroville police. There had been a disturbing series of armed robberies in town, and the chief of police began an operation intended to catch the robbers. It was for this reason that Halber, one night, found himself with an Oroville cop known as "Action Jackson," armed with riot shotguns, and concealed in the back storage room of the Bent Prop Liquor Store. Other officers were similarly concealed in the other liquor stores in town.

As Halber awaited the possible appearance of the armed robbers, he smiled to himself and thought, *Won't they be surprised.*

Hours passed and nothing happened. Then just before midnight, a call came over the radio. An armed robbery had just occurred at the Sunshine Tavern in the old part of town. Halber and Jackson sprinted for the police car hidden behind the store. Within seconds, they were speeding, code-three, toward the scene of the crime. As they traveled, lights flashing, siren screaming, they received more information over the radio. The suspect, wearing a black T-shirt with a pink logo on the front, had held the tavern's owner at knife point and fled on foot, his pockets stuffed with cash.

Halber, in the meantime, was thinking ahead. He knew that the Sunshine Tavern was about two blocks south of the Feather River. If the suspect fled north, the river would pose a barrier to him. However, a well-traveled trail followed the edge of the river, a trail that would be deserted at night and would provide a hidden and relatively safe escape route for a suspect fleeing on foot. With this in mind, Halber had Action Jackson drop him off near the river.

Halber set out on foot, arriving at the trail a quarter mile upstream from where he would expect the suspect to appear had he headed for the river. With powerful Streamlight flashlight in hand, but switched off, Halber slipped down the night-darkened trail. He had gone but a short distance when a shadowy figure appeared. Halber slipped into dense foliage beside the trail.

As a man drew nearer, Halber studied his approach. Whoever it was obviously was not out for a hike, but was proceeding slowly and warily. Halber was certain he had his man. Concealed a mere arm's length from the trail, Halber prepared himself for the action to follow.

Waiting until the man was but five feet from him, Halber suddenly lit him up and blinded him with his flashlight. In the two seconds that followed, several things happened almost simultaneously: Halber noted the man's black T-shirt with pink logo. He noted that the man had no weapons in hand. He lunged for the man, grabbing him and shouting, "Police!" The man lost control of his bladder. Halber took him to the ground, pinning him, and cuffing his hands behind his back.

With the suspect subdued, Halber reached for his radio.

"OPD. . . .Fish and Game two-one-ten . . . I have your two-eleven suspect in custody."

Within seconds several police units arrived, among them Action Jackson.

"Halber, you did good," said Jackson.

The armed robbery suspect went to jail in the back of Jackson's cage car, and Halber went to the police station and wrote his report.

When his report was submitted, Halber went home and crawled into bed. He was barely asleep when his bedside phone rang.

"James? OPD here," said a familiar feminine voice. "Your gizmo's beeping."

Halber leaped out of bed, threw on his uniform and gun belt and dashed out the door. Having planned for this weeks earlier, he knew exactly what to do. He knew that the gravel road leading from the back gate of the hatchery was about a half-mile long, joining the pavement at the top of a high bluff overlooking the river. Halber raced to the bluff. There he waited, blocking the road and blacked out. Stepping out of his patrol vehicle, he studied the road below through his binoculars.

About 15 minutes later, he spotted a vehicle coming his way with its lights out. As it approached, Halber again prepared himself for action.

***

Sidney Bogman was congratulating himself as he crept along through the darkness, cheerful over having apparently pulled off yet another successful gasoline heist. But he was no longer just a petty criminal/gasoline thief, for of late he had begun trying his hand at residential burglaries. At that very moment, in fact, on the passenger-side floor of his pickup was a pillow slip containing expensive jewelry and other loot he had taken earlier that night from the home of an 82-year-old woman.

As the road began to climb toward the top of the bluff, he was in fine humor. But upon reaching the top, his good humor turned instantly to terror when another vehicle charged toward him, blinding him with bright lights.

***

Halber stopped bumper to bumper with Bogman's blacked-out vehicle and directed the beam of his roof-mounted spotlight into the vehicle's cab. He then slipped out, flashlight in hand, and hurried through his own headlights to the passenger side window of Bogman's pickup.

"State game warden," shouted Halber, directing his flashlight beam inside. "Keep your hands where I can see them."

The already blinded and violently trembling Bogman complied.

"I'm sorry, I'm sorry," cried Bogman. "I know I shouldn't have done it."

Halber directed his light into the rear of the pickup and spotted two 55-gallon drums.

"Are those full of hatchery gas?" Halber asked.

"Yes," cried Bogman. "I'm sorry."

Halber removed Bogman from the pickup, handcuffed him behind his back, read him his rights, and seat-belted him in the passenger seat of the patrol vehicle. Halber then did a quick search of Bogman's pickup. Discovering the pillow slip containing obviously stolen property, he asked Bogman about it. Bogman had nothing to say.

Halber locked Bogman's pickup, then drove the man to the Oroville Police Station. There Halber plugged in the black light and directed the dark beam onto Bogman's hands as the dispatcher and the duty sergeant looked on. Bogman's hands lit up like bright neon. His right palm glowed a brilliant green, and his right thumb, which he had obviously used to turn on the gas pump switch, glowed bright red.

Halber thoroughly photographed Bogman's hands, then placed the man in the police station's tiny holding cell. Halber then retrieved the pillow slip and its contents from his patrol rig. Upon seeing the bulging pillow slip, the duty sergeant was immediately interested.

"We had a burglary call a few hours ago," he said, examining the contents of the pillow case. "Some guy reported seeing a man coming out of his neighbor's house. His neighbor is an old lady, and the man was carrying something in some kind of sack. We investigated and learned that the old lady was missing jewelry, some silver dollars, a camera and some other stuff. This has to be it."

As dawn was breaking, Halber wearily wrote his second arrest report of the night. He then loaded Bogman into the patrol rig and drove him to Butte County Jail. After booking Bogman, Halber left him in the booking cage and drove home, crawled into bed and slept as though he had been drugged.

The hatchery people were happy to learn of Halber's arrest of the gas bandit, and an elderly woman was overjoyed with the return of her stolen property, which included her deceased husband's wedding band. These things provided Halber with pleasant memories over the years that followed, but what entertained him most was recalling the words of the OPD sergeant when the man realized that Halber had made two separate and unassisted felony arrests that night.

"One burglar and one armed robber in one night," the sergeant had said with a smile. "Not bad for a fish cop!"

Fuzz Face, Snake Eyes and Fu Manchu

It was crowding midnight when the bear stalked into the Lakes Basin Campground. He padded silently through the maze of tents, tables and parked vehicles, guided by his nose, ignoring the pervasive man-scent. It wasn't the first time he had raided the camp for the easy meals to be found there, but this foray would prove to be his last.

Not everyone in the campground was yet asleep on that night, and among those who were awake and witnessed the bear's arrival were three rough-looking characters slouched in camp chairs around a fire pit. Not only did they watch the bear arrive, they had been expecting him. In conversations earlier that day with the camp host, one Charles Rupp, they had learned that the bear was a nightly visitor and had become a substantial nuisance, at least to Rupp.

"He tore up a camp trailer near here last week, and he keeps me awake all night," Rupp had said. "I want him out of here, one way or another."

Rupp did everything but wink at the three men, who were obviously hunters of a sort, and there was no doubt in their minds that Rupp wanted them to kill the bear when it arrived that night. One of them happened to have a bear tag, and it appeared to be a great opportunity. To prepare for the bear's coming, the men put out bait to attract the animal to their campsite. They poured bacon grease on the concrete rim of the fire pit, and they punched holes in three cans of pork and beans and placed them on the ground nearby. When night came, they sat by the fire, passed around a bottle of Jack Daniels and waited.

However, when the bear arrived, he ambled directly to the trash dumpsters that were but a few feet away from Rupp's trailer. Standing on his hind legs, he pried at the heavy steel lid on one of the dumpsters. When this didn't work, he scrambled up on top of the dumpster, hooked claws and paws under one corner of the lid, and with strength several times that of the strongest man alive, he pulled upward. With a groan of tortured metal, the steel gave way and rolled back like the tin lid of a sardine can.

Rupp watched this amazing feat from his trailer a mere 15 feet away, and he saw the bear squeeze through the new opening and disappear within. Rupp then noted the arrival of one of the three men he had spoken to earlier in hopes they would eliminate his bear problem. The man had long hair, a dense tangle of facial hair, carried a rifle, and he was clearly intoxicated. With a wary eye on the dumpster, Rupp immediately stepped out and spoke to him.

"You can't use a rifle here in the campground," he said, and for the benefit of others whom he was sure were listening, he added, "You need to do this legally."

Fuzz Face swayed on his feet, blinked a few times, and reluctantly staggered back to his camp. Rupp was then approached by several campers worried for their own safety as well as the safety of the bear.

"You need to call the sheriff," one of them implored. "That guy is drunk, armed and dangerous."

Rupp made a show of using his telephone. He indeed called the sheriff's office, but he neglected to mention Fuzz Face and his rifle. He reported only that there was a bear in his dumpster. But bears were always in dumpsters and trash cans in the Lakes

Basin area, and though it was a problem, the sheriff's office viewed it as Fish and Game's problem.

Soon after the arrival of Fuzz Face and the concerned campers, the bear abandoned the dumpster and headed into the forest. But when things quieted down, he returned, and the thumping and bumping and the clatter of cans and bottles inside the dumpster resumed.

Back at Fuzz Face's campsite, the dominant of the three men there was a tall, villainous-looking character in a floppy-brimmed camo bush hat and a large, drooping Fu Manchu mustache. Upon noting the obvious return of the bear, this man slipped into his tent and emerged bearing a compound bow with an attached quiver of razor-edged broadhead hunting arrows.

"Bring a light," said Fu Manchu, addressing the third member of the trio, a slender man with close-set, dead-looking eyes that gave him a distinctive snake-like appearance. Fu Manchu and Snake Eyes then set out through the trees for the dumpster. Fuzz Face and Jack Daniels brought up the rear.

Due to his unsteady gait, Fuzz Face lagged some distance behind the others. He encountered two other campers out gathering firewood despite the late hour.

"What's going on?" one of them inquired.

"There's a bear over there in the trash. We're going to get it," said Fuzz Face. Then he added, "You're not going to tell on us are you?"

"Well, yes," said the camper. "We are going to tell on you. We're gonna call Fish and Game."

Fuzz Face blinked a few times as his whiskey-numbed brain processed this information. He then turned, bottle in hand, and stumbled after his companions. He arrived at the dumpster in time to see Fu Manchu fit a broadhead onto his bowstring and arrow rest while Snake Eyes directed a bright flashlight beam on the dumpster. Then the bear appeared, climbing out of the dumpster, and Fu Manchu drew the bow and released. The arrow struck the bear with a distinctive thump, slicing a destructive path through the animal's heart and lungs. The stricken bear grunted once, fell to the ground and died.

Fu Manchu then turned to Rupp's darkened trailer, spotted the glow of Rupp's lighted cigarette within and gave him a thumbs-up signal. Although Rupp had witnessed everything, he did not respond. Within 15 minutes, Fu Manchu and his two friends had the bear loaded into the back of their Jeep, and then they drove out of the campground, headed for town.

***

California Fish and Game Warden Steve Ulrich got the call at around noon the following day. It came through dispatch in Sacramento, and they provided him the name and phone number of the RP, reporting party. It appeared that someone had shot a bear in a dumpster. Although archery bear season was open, it was against state law to shoot a bear anywhere near a dumpster, and it was illegal to shoot one at night. Ulrich picked up the phone and dialed the RP.

The RP went through it all, how he and his friend had been gathering firewood when they encountered the three armed men hurrying toward the dumpsters by the camp host's trailer. He related his conversation with the hairy-faced individual.

"I don't believe it!" said the RP. "I told them I was going to call Fish and Game, and they killed the bear anyway. Really dumb! We heard the arrow hit it, and we heard the bear groan, and we walked over and saw it on the ground dead. And this morning, there was a lot of blood by the dumpster. The camp host was cleaning it up."

Ulrich extracted every bit of information he could from the man, including a description of the red Jeep in which the suspects had departed the scene, and then arranged to meet with him at the campground. Soon thereafter, Ulrich pulled away from his home in Portola and headed for Lakes Basin.

When Ulrich arrived at the campground, two Sierra County deputies were already there. Another witness had apparently complained to the sheriff's office about a drunk man with a rifle. Ulrich spoke briefly with the deputies, and then contacted the camp host. Charles Rupp was not pleased to see him and was obviously a bit nervous over something. But he admitted telling the three men that he wanted the bear dead and that it was keeping him awake every night. Despite the fact that Rupp added that he had told the three men he wanted it done legally, Ulrich and a deputy who was with him correctly concluded at this point that Rupp had been part of the problem.

Rupp spoke of his conversation with the hairy-faced, rifle-toting man, and proudly announced that he had sent the man back to his campsite.

"Did you see or hear the bear being killed?" asked Ulrich.

"No," said Rupp. "I went to bed and slept through the whole thing." Ulrich then regarded the picture window on Rupp's trailer a mere 15 feet from the bloody dumpster, and his suspicion of the man multiplied.

"I thought you said it kept you awake all night," said the deputy.

"Well, most of the night," said Rupp.

Ulrich now examined the dumpster and noted blood and claw marks both inside and outside of the dumpster, but it was obvious that someone had cleaned up much of the blood on the ground. Ulrich was certain that the bear had died here.

"Did you clean up the blood?" Ulrich inquired, turning to Rupp.

"I cleaned it up," said Rupp, and Ulrich was annoyed that the man had disturbed his crime scene. He was also much annoyed that Rupp, a camp host for the U.S. Forest Service, had failed to report the crime.

Ulrich thoroughly photographed the dumpster with its blood and claw marks, and he took shots of the cleaned-up ground as well. Rupp was becoming more and more disturbed.

Ulrich now turned his attention to the tents and camping gear remaining at Campsite 10, the one that had been occupied by the three suspects. Two tents stood near a small travel trailer with no license plate, and a green parachute was stretched above the table as an awning. Ulrich immediately spotted the opened cans of pork and beans and the bacon grease, and he knew instantly their purpose. He photographed this bait, then moved on to the tents.

For officer safety purposes, Ulrich looked inside the tents. He needed to be sure that no one was sleeping inside, and he wanted to know whether any weapons might be accessible to the suspects upon their return. In one of the tents, Ulrich noted a single broadhead arrow and a set of bear tags. He quickly jotted down the name Luther Bunts from the bear tags.

A quick look inside the travel trailer revealed a sawed-off, double-barreled, 12 gage shotgun. Ulrich applied his tape measure to the shortened barrel and found it to be just barely legal.

While he was inspecting the campground, several campers approached Ulrich and corroborated the earlier reports that the men from Campsite 10 had indeed killed a bear in the dumpster the night before. Ulrich arranged to get written statements from all of them.

Because the campground was in Tahoe National Forest, it was the U.S. Forest Service's turf. Ulrich therefore decided to radio Tom Rowland, an enforcement officer with the Forest Service, and apprise him of the situation. This turned out to be a great move on Ulrich's part, for 15 minutes after Rowland got the information about three suspects in a red Jeep, he encountered them. He had stopped to buy gas in Portola when he spotted the Jeep parked there and one of the three men, a tall man with a large, drooping Fu Manchu mustache, approached him.

"Hey, man, I shot a bear this morning and I need to get it validated," said Fu Manchu. Rowland recognized the man as a local criminal, a convicted felon and wife beater who had narrowly escaped death one night when he drew a handgun on a deputy sheriff.

Rowland told him he would try to reach a game warden by radio, and as Rowland reached for his microphone, Fu Manchu rejoined his companions back at the red Jeep.

"Hey, Steve, I think I have your suspects," said Rowland into his mike. "There're three of 'em in a red Jeep, and one of them wants a bear validated."

"Great!" said Ulrich. "We need to get them back to their campsite. We have felony violations here."

"What felony violations?" came a voice behind Rowland. Rowland turned and was shocked to see that Fu Manchu had returned in time to hear part of Ulrich's transmission. "What felony violations?" the man repeated. "I've been clean for over two years now."

Thinking fast, Rowland said, "Oh, this doesn't pertain to you. They've got some other guys stopped up by Davis Lake."

But it was clear that Fu Manchu wasn't convinced. Rowland now told him that the wardens were tied up and that one of them would telephone him later if he would leave a number. The man did provide a phone number, and he told Rowland that he had taken the bear to Wiggins' Trading Post in Chilcoot. He then slipped behind the wheel of the Jeep, cast one last suspicious glance back at Rowland, then drove away with his friends. Rowland allowed them a good lead, then followed through the rolling sage and pine-forested hills. He stayed well back, catching just a glimpse of the Jeep now and then. He stayed with them for over 10 miles before they gave him the slip. He advised Ulrich by radio.

"I lost 'em in Graeagle," said Rowland, "But I think they're heading your way."

In the meantime, Ulrich had provided the name he had observed on the bear tag in the tent, Luther Bunt, to one of the deputies still at the campground. The deputy had run the name through dispatch for outstanding warrants or criminal history. They learned that Bunt had done hard time for a number of crimes. It seemed that Fuzz Face, as they would come to refer to him, was a convicted felon. Additionally, he was in the habit of fighting with cops, so he had therefore earned "violent offender" status.

Armed with the information that at least two of the three suspects were felons, Ulrich and the two deputies set about preparing an appropriate ambush for them. They selected a place near the entrance to the campground where they would execute a high-risk stop. The suspects would be taken down at gunpoint.

***

Fu Manchu nervously stroked his drooping mustache as he drove along, the Jeep racing southbound on Highway 89. He had a campsite full of gear that needed retrieving, but he was worried. He sensed a trap. What could he do? Even if he abandoned the gear and didn't return to camp, the game wardens would sooner or later get to him anyway. But the nearer he got to the campground, the more nervous he grew.

When they were about a mile from the campground entrance, he suddenly swerved the Jeep onto the shoulder and braked to a stop.

"I'm gonna walk the rest of the way in case something's up," he said, stepping out. "You drive, Luther."

Fuzz Face dutifully walked around to the driver's side and climbed in. Fu Manchu stalked off across a sage flat to a forest of pines and firs that would hide him all the way to the campground. Snake Eyes remained in the back seat.

Fuzz Face drove the remaining mile, then turned onto the campground road. As he approached the first of the campsites, he rounded a nearly blind curve and slammed on the brakes, for there, blocking the roadway, was a sheriff's patrol vehicle and a green Fish and Game pickup, red lights aimed directly at his face. Shielded behind the open doors of the vehicles were one game warden and one deputy sheriff armed with semi-automatic pistols. Leaning across the hood of the sheriff's unit was a second deputy with an ugly-looking 12 gage riot shotgun. Fuzz Face was quick to note that all three weapons were pointed directly at him.

"STATE OFFICER!" shouted Ulrich. "KEEP YOUR HANDS WHERE WE CAN SEE THEM! NOW, DRIVER . . . TURN THE ENGINE OFF AND DROP THE KEYS OUT THE WINDOW!" Fuzz Face, with trembling hands, complied. "NOW, KEEP YOUR HANDS UP AND STEP OUT!"

Ulrich soon had both men out of the Jeep and flat on their bellies on the pavement. Seconds later, both men were handcuffed behind their backs.

Ulrich was puzzled over the missing third suspect. He asked the two handcuffed men about it, and both denied that there had been a third man with them. Ulrich then reached for his radio mike and called Rowland.

"Are you sure there were three suspects in the Jeep?" he asked. "There are just two of them now."

"There were definitely three when I last saw them," said Rowland.

Ulrich then searched the Jeep, noting fresh blood and bear hair within, and recovered a compound bow with arrows. He then searched the camp, seized the double-barreled shotgun into evidence and found a loaded Marlin, lever-action .30-30 rifle under a jacket in one of the tents. As he carried the rifle and shotgun to his patrol vehicle, Fuzz Face spotted him.

"Am I gonna get my rifle back?" Fuzz Face inquired.

"It's not likely, since you're a convicted felon," said Ulrich.

Ulrich then separated the two men, read them their rights and questioned them. The warden was surprised when both suspects readily fingered the missing third man, stating that he had shot the bear in the dumpster during the night. Both suspects also said that the camp host had put them up to it.

Soon thereafter, the mystery of the missing third suspect was solved when a camper approached Ulrich and said, "You know the third guy you're looking for? He's here. He was just talking to the camp host a few minutes ago."

Ulrich wasted no time thanking the man, then set out for Rupp's trailer.

"Yeah, I saw him," said Rupp. "He asked me what was going on."

"What did you tell him?" asked Ulrich.

As if to prove the old adage among wardens, *We only catch the dumb ones*, Rupp readily replied, "I told him you had his friends in handcuffs and that he'd better disappear. He's out there in the woods somewhere."

By warning the suspect, Rupp had committed a clear case of interfering with and impeding Ulrich's investigation. Ulrich made mental note of this, then made several radio calls. Soon he had a fine manhunt in progress. Even deputies from adjoining counties showed up to help, and a Highway Patrol helicopter was on its way. However after an hour of hard searching, Fu Manchu remained at large.

Then the searchers got a break: A camper caught a glimpse of the man in heavy brush, and about that time a Plumas County K-9 unit arrived. The officers then set out in a skirmish line with the dog handler in the middle. The large German shepherd barked excitedly.

"COME OUT OR WE'RE GONNA SEND IN THE DOG!" shouted the handler.

Fu Manchu, who had been bitten in the crotch by an attack dog earlier in his criminal career, had no desire to experience it again. Without hesitation he popped up like a jack-in-the-box, hands high over his head.

"HANG ON TO THE DOG!" he cried. "I GIVE UP!"

Fu Manchu proved to be as talkative as his two friends, and Ulrich, by means of a skillful interrogation, soon had the whole story.

In the meantime, a California Highway Patrol officer had arrived. Ulrich and the deputies had detected alcohol on Fuzz Face's breath, and they had determined that he had been driving on a suspended license. Fuzz Face flunked his field sobriety test, and he blew a breath test that revealed a blood alcohol level twice what the law allowed. He would have been booked into county jail anyway, but now there would be a DUI added to the long list of charges. The Highway Patrol officer transported both Fuzz Face and Snake Eyes to jail. Fu Manchu soon ended up there as well.

With what appeared to be a slam-dunk case against the three men, Ulrich still had the task of completing his investigation and tying up a variety of loose ends. He retrieved the bear from the cold-storage locker at Wiggins' Trading Post, took blood and hair samples from the Jeep, the dumpster and from the bear itself, and he put evidence tags on the seized equipment. Fu Manchu had falsified the information on his bear tag, stating that the bear had been killed at a location over 15 miles from the actual kill site, and he had claimed that it had been taken during legal hunting hours. This falsification of a document would be another charge against him.

But the most serious charge against the three men was that of conspiracy, the act of conspiring among themselves to commit a violation of state law. In California, this was a serious charge, a felony. Ulrich compiled an impressive collection of witness statements, reports written by himself, the deputies and the Highway Patrol officer, photographs of the dead bear, the damaged and bloody dumpster and photographs from a camera Ulrich had found in the Jeep. The latter photographs were of Fu Manchu posing with the killed bear arranged in a sitting position in a grocery store shopping cart as though taking a ride. All of these things Ulrich combined in a beautifully bound and indexed package, which he presented to the Sierra County district attorney.

In the end, the court sentences of the three suspects were somewhat disappointing, which was often true with Fish and Game cases. Judges accustomed to rape, murder and armed robbery cases tended to view wildlife related crimes as minor. But as for the convicted violators of this case, the judge certainly got their attention. Snake Eyes got off with a stiff fine for his part, Fu Manchu lost his equipment and did a full month in jail, and Fuzz Face, due mainly to his being a felon in possession of a firearm, was sent back to San Quentin for a year.

But the best satisfaction Ulrich experienced related to the bear-in-a-dumpster case came when he and Rowland paid one last visit to Charles Rupp, the conniving camp host who was perhaps the man most responsible for the entire incident. Rupp, with good reason, came to the door looking highly nervous.

"Mr. Rupp," said Ulrich. "You're under arrest for aiding, abetting and encouraging others in the commission of a crime, for obstructing and delaying a peace officer, and for aiding and abetting a fleeing felon."

Rupp began to tremble, fear and desperate regret burning in the pit of his stomach like a hot stone.

Repeat Offenders

Veteran salmon poacher Gilbert "Bert" Coggsdale squinted in the midnight darkness and scanned Upper Matthews Riffle with wary eyes. He saw no one, concluding that he still had his favorite stretch of the Feather River all to himself.

Satisfied for the moment, he flipped back the bail back on his heavy spin-fishing outfit, reared back with his rod and flung a weighted cluster of large treble hooks into a deep drift that he knew to contain salmon. Two sweeping jerks with the rod later, he felt the hooks bite into flesh, and the fight was on.

Snagged through its dorsal fin, the big fish fought valiantly, racing first upriver then down. But seven minutes later Coggsdale dragged it, flopping, onto a gravel bar and killed it with a rock.

Fighting the big fish had taken Coggsdale to the far side of the river from where his wife had dropped him off a half hour earlier. Now it was nearly time for her to pick him up, so he tied the fish to a rope and began dragging it back across the swift-moving stretch of knee-deep riffle. Out of habit, he scanned the far bank for any sign of wardens as he slogged along in the moonlight.

Near the middle of the river was a small, willow-covered island that provided easy walking for about 30 feet along one of its sides. Coggsdale arrived at the island and headed along the path, willow branches brushing his left shoulder.

Suddenly terror struck a hammer-blow to his heart as something big sprang from the willows and grabbed him. He yelped as strong arms pinned him, and he could do nothing but gasp for breath.

"State game warden!" growled a voice in his ear. "Don't even think about running!"

But Coggsdale could not have even stood, let alone run, his legs having been reduced to Jello.

Lieutenant James Halber, California Department of Fish and Game, loosened his hold on the man and illuminated his face with a small flashlight.

"Bert? Not you again!" said Halber. Seconds passed before the man was able to reply.

"Yeah, Jim . . . it's me," gasped Coggsdale. "Sally got fish-hungry . . . Looks like you got me again."

"Well, come on," said Halber, snatching up the salmon rope. "You know the drill."

Upon reaching the bank, Halber cited Coggsdale for illegally taking salmon at night and by snagging.

"How's Sally doing?" said Halber as Coggsdale signed the citation.

"She's doing okay," said Coggsdale. "I think that's her coming now."

Approaching headlights did indeed turn out to be Coggsdale's wife and occasional accomplice in crime, as she was on this night. Upon her arrival in a battered pickup, she stepped out and said, "Hello, Jim. I see you've got him again!"

Halber always marveled over Sally Coggsdale's polite and cheerful attitude toward the game wardens. Her husband was the same way. Halber had cost them thousands of dollars in fines, having arrested Bert Coggsdale numerous times, perhaps more times than any other violator, usually for fishing violations. Halber had even searched every inch of their home one time on a search warrant, and yet they treated him like a family friend.

And so it was on this night. When Halber was done with him, Coggsdale climbed into the pickup with his wife and bade Halber a cheerful farewell . . . despite the fact that he, Coggsdale, was facing a stiff fine and was in desperate need of a change of underwear.

When Coggsdale was gone, Halber found himself thinking back over his long association with the man. Actually, Halber's first memory of Coggsdale was nearly 20 years earlier, as a smiling, cheerful 14-year-old, freshly captured from snagging salmon in the fish ladder at the Feather River Hatchery in Oroville.

On this occasion, Halber had given the boy a serious chewing out and had sent him on his way. But the warning had apparently made little impression on him, for Halber caught him a week later doing the same thing.

From then on, rarely six months would pass without Halber or one of the other wardens encountering Coggsdale abusing the fishing regulations in some way. When he turned 18, his frequent brushes with the law became expensive, but he was always cheerful and cooperative when captured, or in court when he was sentenced, and he never seemed to hold anything against the wardens or judges.

Coggsdale never resisted arrest, but he would occasionally make a run for it. One dark night Halber had spotted a car hidden near the river behind the hatchery. Halber correctly concluded that someone was snagging salmon from the infamous "Pipe Hole," a popular poacher destination at the time.

Because Halber did not know how many suspects were involved, and because they could have salmon hidden along the river, Halber chose not to approach them on the river. Instead, he would wait for a "package deal," when the salmon and the poachers were all loaded in the vehicle and headed for home.

Halber took up a position on the bluffs above the river, on the only road leading up from the river at that point. An hour later, he spotted the vehicle coming out. Waiting until it topped out on the bluff, Halber hit it with his emergency lights, intending to make a head-on stop. But without hesitation, the driver accelerated, swerving up and over a curb and around the patrol vehicle. Gaining the road behind the patrol vehicle, the driver raced away through a residential district.

Halber wheeled around and gave chase, red light ablaze, siren wailing, gas pedal to the floor. As he was coming up behind the vehicle, something large sailed out the passenger window. Halber recognized it as a large salmon. Then another flew out . . . and another . . . a total of six. One struck a mailbox, knocking it askew. Another struck a parked car.

Soon, however, the suspects ran out of road, speeding up on a dead end. The driver tried to turn around, but Halber pinned him in. Stepping from the patrol vehicle, flashlight held high in his left hand, Halber made a careful approach to the driver's window. Directing the flashlight beam inside, Halber was greeted with a smile from a familiar face.

"Hello, Jim! Guess it's not my lucky night!"

Accompanying Coggsdale on that night was a weasel of a man named Lester Tubbs. It was Tubbs, in fact, who had tossed six evidence salmon out the passenger window of Coggsdale's car. Halber had later recovered five of the fish.

The presence of Tubbs with Coggsdale on that night was no surprise to Halber, for Tubbs had been nailed by wardens almost as many times as Coggsdale. The two, in fact, had become inseparable. While their crimes usually involved fish, they occasionally dabbled in deer poaching.

One afternoon Halber received a tip from one of Coggsdale's neighbors reporting that Coggsdale and another man had carried a dead deer into his house. A description of the other man led Halber to conclude that it was most likely Tubbs, who lived on the third floor of an old hotel building in Oroville.

Halber decided to pay Coggsdale a knock-and-talk visit, but not before he assigned two reserve wardens to positions from which they could keep an eye on Tubbs. The old hotel building where Tubbs lived was about 10 minutes travel from Coggsdale's house south of Oroville.

Just before dark, two Fish and Game patrol rigs pulled up in front of Coggsdale's house. Halber and Warden Leonard Blissenbach went to the door. Their knock was answered immediately by Coggsdale.

"Hello, Bert," said Halber. "I guess you know why we're here."

"No, Jim," said Coggsdale. "I don't know why you're here. What's the problem?"

"Well, we got a report that you have deer meat in your house."

"Deer meat? I don't have any deer meat!"

"Well, these reports are often false, but we have to investigate," said Halber. "If you let us take a quick look inside, we'll be on our way."

Halber knew Coggsdale to be the type of outlaw who claims innocence to the bitter end. So Halber was not surprised when Coggsdale answered, "Sure. Come on in. I've got nothing to hide."

The wardens entered the house, and Halber exchanged friendly greetings with Sally Coggsdale, who was at work at the kitchen sink.

"I just have to take a quick look in your refrigerator, Sally," said Halber.

"Go ahead," she said. "I know you're just doing your job."

Halber checked the refrigerator and freezer and found nothing. Blissenbach, however, had better luck.

"Jim, you need to come in here," said Blissenbach, calling out through a bathroom door. Halber joined him, and Blissenbach pointed to the bathtub. Wrapped in a bloody sheet were the roughly butchered parts of about half a deer.

"Guess you got me again," said Coggsdale with a grin. He then went on to claim that the deer had been a road-kill he had brought home. The wardens, however, thought otherwise.

Blissenbach wrote Coggsdale a citation for illegal possession of deer meat, almost knowing Coggsdale's address and driver's license number by heart. Halber lugged the deer meat out to his patrol vehicle, then returned and addressed Coggsdale again.

"Bert! Did Lester Tubbs have anything to do with this? There's some of this deer missing."

"No," said Coggsdale adamantly. "Lester had nothing to do with this."

"Okay," said Halber, moving close and looking the man square in the eyes. "Now, I need your word on something. I need your word of honor that you will not call Lester Tubbs for at least a half hour after we leave."

"Sure," said Coggsdale, raising his left hand as though in solemn oath. "You've got my word of honor. I won't call him at all tonight."

"Thank you, Bert," said Halber. "We'll be in touch."

The wardens then departed. Coggsdale watched them drive away, then dove for his telephone.

At that exact minute, Reserve Warden Jack Teagarden was standing in the gathering darkness beside a large trash dumpster behind the old hotel building in Oroville. About four minutes later, as Teagarden was peering up at a rickety fire escape leading down from the third floor, the third floor door burst open and out hurried Lester Tubbs carrying something heavy in a plastic trash bag. He clambered down the stairs with it and was just about to fling it into the dumpster when out stepped a very large game warden in full uniform.

"Good evening, Lester," said Teagarden. "How's it going?"

Among the deer parts in Tubbs' plastic bag, the wardens found both sides of the animal's rib cage. One side bore a neat little .22 caliber bullet hole.

Following the conviction of Coggsdale and Tubbs for taking a deer out of season, Coggsdale apparently retired from fish and wildlife poaching. He entered a darker period of his life marked by periodic arrests for drug sales and manufacturing. He did jail time more than once, and the wardens lost track of him.

It was one night, years after the deer-in-the-bathtub case, that Halber decided to spend a night watching for salmon poachers on the Feather River. His plan was to stake out a problem area, the Fish Barrier Dam adjacent to the Feather River Hatchery. This dam was the end of the road for upstream migrating king salmon and steelhead. The large pool below the dam was therefore jammed with hundreds of highly visible salmon and steelhead, a poacher's dream. Even though the wardens kept a close eye on the place, many poachers just couldn't resist.

Halber took up a position on high ground, on the hatchery side of the river, overlooking the Fish Barrier Dam. Below him was one edge of the hatchery, consisting of roads, a parking lot, the fish ladder and an observation platform. But Halber was most interested in the opposite side of the river where the shoreline was a jumble of huge boulders on bedrock.

It was on the opposite side that poachers would most likely appear. They would walk in, a quarter mile or so from town, on a gravel road between the river and the railroad tracks. Upon reaching the dam, they would make their way down the steep bank through the boulders to the water's edge where they would cast into the dense concentration of fish. The wardens had made hundreds of arrests there over the years, and yet poachers still appeared there with regularity. The worst of the illegal activity occurred there at night.

And so it was that Halber settled in for what would probably be a long wait, night vision scope in hand. Because the hatchery side of the river was illuminated by streetlights, a little light made it to the opposite shore. It was enough light that Halber, with his night scope, could make out every detail on the far bank.

Hours passed with no activity. Every three minutes or so, Halber scanned the far bank and the gravel road leading to the dam. It wasn't until long after midnight that he spotted four dark forms hurrying along the road toward the dam. As they drew nearer, Halber could see that they were carrying fishing rods. Halber reached for his hand-set radio and made a call.

It was good fortune that Warden Blissenbach and Reserve Warden Ron Hastings were available. They had just cleared the Butte County Jail after booking two rough-looking suspects for possession of a sizeable stash of methamphetamines, packaged for sale, in their car on the Oroville Wildlife Area. Halber explained the situation, and the two wardens immediately headed for the river. Ten minutes later, they had parked the patrol rig and were walking in on the gravel road.

In the meantime, Halber had watched the four snagging suspects reach the water, make casts and hook salmon. He had then marveled at how fast the suspects horsed the big fish in on what had to be very heavy gear. Each of the four suspects appeared to catch a big salmon within just a few minutes of their arrival, then, to Halber's surprise, all four of them gathered up their fish and fishing gear and started up through the boulders to leave the area.

Halber radioed Blissenbach, explaining the problem. It was clear that the suspects would make it up to the gravel road before the two wardens could arrive, and Halber knew that if the wardens encountered the suspects on the road, the suspects would scatter like quail. At best the wardens would catch one or two of them.

But Halber had an idea. A few minutes earlier, Officer Al Fawcett of the California State Police had heard the wardens' radio traffic and had called Halber to ask if he could assist. Fawcett was but a few hundred yards away at the main hatchery building. Halber had initially asked him to stand by, but Halber now called him again.

"Al, we need your help. We need you to drive in over here where I am and shine your spotlight around like you're making a routine check of the area. But if you spot the suspects on the other side of the river, keep your light moving and act like you don't see them."

"Will do," said Fawcett, and seconds later he was there, traveling slowly, his spotlight sweeping back and forth.

The suspects were then about halfway up to the gravel road, but upon seeing a police car shining a light around, they did exactly what Halber had hoped they would do: They dove under a huge boulder and vanished, becoming "a package deal" for the wardens.

"You're doing great, Al. Keep it up," said Halber into his radio. Fawcett kept searching with his spotlight, and the suspects remained hidden under the boulder.

Soon thereafter, Blissenbach and Hastings arrived, and Halber directed them, by radio, to the right boulder. Blissenbach carefully circled the boulder one direction, and Hastings came around the other way, then they lit up the suspects with their bright flashlights.

"They were tangled up under that rock like a ball of snakes," Hastings later told Halber in his colorful way. "And what do you think one of them said?"

"I don't know," said Halber. "What did he say?"

Hastings grinned. "When we lit them up and told them not to move, one of them called out, "Is that you, Jim?"

Swift Justice

A fall evening in the oak-forested hills of Yuba County.

Jason Robert Hook, a long, narrow string bean of a man, rested his .22 rifle on a fence post and took a quick look around. He then bent at the waist, lowered his head and settled his cheek against the rifle's polished stock. Peering down the barrel, he brought the sights to bear on the largest of several wild turkeys feeding in a forest clearing.

The fact that it was illegal to shoot turkeys with a .22 rifle was of little concern to Hook, of no more concern than the additional facts that turkey season was closed, he lacked a hunting license, and the bird was on posted private property.

Hook aimed for the base of the turkey's neck, and he squeezed the trigger. The rifle popped, and the tiny slug zipped to its mark. The turkey hen flopped and thrashed for a few seconds, her spinal cord severed, then she lay still.

Hook again glanced around, then with his long legs he stepped easily over the barbed wire fence. Seconds later, he had retrieved the dead bird, returned over the fence and was back on Rankin Road. He set off with long strides down the country road, rifle in one hand, the illegally killed turkey in the other.

As he passed one of the few houses, its owner shook his head in wonder as Hook strode by. *What a fool. Doesn't he know about game wardens?* The man then reached for his phone. A turkey hunter himself, but a legal one, he had the CalTIP number close at hand. The CalTIP dispatcher took his information and thanked him for the call.

***

Fish and Game Warden Sean Pirtle peered through his tripod-mounted spotting scope, watching as a large king salmon fought for its life. A fisherman in an aluminum boat had intentionally snagged the big fish and was fighting it on heavy tackle. A metal jig bearing a large treble hook was lodged near the fish's dorsal fin. From another vantage point a half mile upriver, Warden Mark Imsdahl, binoculars to his eyes, was watching the same unfolding violation.

The Feather River was full of the big fish, the spawning season in full swing, and poaching was a constant problem for the wardens. It was for this reason that Warden Pirtle had left his regular patrol area in Yuba County on that day to assist the wardens in Butte County with their salmon problems at the infamous "Outlet Hole" near Oroville.

The big fish was tiring, its strength nearly depleted, and as it surfaced, 20 feet from the boat, its back was briefly out of water and exposed to view.

"Did you see that?" said Imsdahl into his radio microphone.

"Yeah," said Pirtle. "It's hooked right behind the dorsal fin."

"And it's an illegal jig," Imsdahl added.

The fish managed one last powerful run, then was slowly dragged to the surface near the boat. A second man in the boat grabbed a large landing net while a third man looked on. As the fish thrashed on the surface, the net man scooped it up and swung it aboard where it flopped violently in the net. Both wardens had got a good look at the fish as it came aboard, and both had again seen the illegal jig hooked fast in the fish's back.

"I'll bet he keeps it," said Imsdahl.

"I'll bet you're right," said Pirtle.

The victorious angler stood grinning for a moment, then raised his right hand and gave high fives to the other two men. Next he produced a hand scale and weighed the big fish, which appeared to the wardens to be about 45 pounds. Had he released the fish at this point, he would have saved himself over a thousand dollars and the loss of his fishing privileges for two years, but instead he struck the fish on the head with a wooden club.

Just then, Pirtle received a radio call from dispatch.

"We have a CalTIP in your district. It just came in. The RP reports seeing a tall skinny man carrying a wild turkey and a .22 rifle, walking down Rankin Road toward Dobbins."

"I'm out of position, and I have a violation in progress," said Pirtle. "Is there a call-back number?"

Pirtle took down the information, then turned his attention again to the three men in the aluminum boat. They had resumed fishing, or more accurately, snagging, and they continued until well after sunset. As darkness was fast approaching, Pirtle made the 10-minute drive to a point near a boat ramp where the suspects would most likely have their vehicle and boat trailer.

The boat ramp was less than a quarter mile upstream from the Outlet Hole, and Pirtle parked his patrol vehicle out of sight on a bluff above it. A single vehicle, a pickup with a boat trailer, was parked near the ramp. From the bluff, Pirtle could see the three suspects in the boat, apparently preparing to depart. But they were having some kind of trouble.

Despite the near-darkness, Pirtle could see that their anchor was stuck. He watched them for over 15 minutes as they tried to dislodge it. By the time they finally got it free, full darkness was upon them. They headed immediately for the ramp. Pirtle left his vehicle, and with flashlight in hand he remained hidden in the darkness. When the boat was less than 20 feet from shore, he walked down to the ramp to meet them.

Just then, someone in the boat turned on a spotlight, sweeping the shoreline. There stood Pirtle, in full view and in full uniform. The boat was just 10 feet from shore, no more than 15 feet from Pirtle, yet the driver immediately threw the engine into reverse and began backing away.

Pirtle lit them up with his powerful Stinger flashlight and shouted.

"STATE GAME WARDEN! COME ASHORE!"

But the driver, who Pirtle recognized as the man who had snagged the big salmon, ignored him, continuing to back away. Pirtle shouted at them repeatedly, motioning for them to come back, but the driver ignored him.

Then the driver spun the boat around, shifted to the forward gear and headed upriver. Pirtle followed them with his light, clearly seeing the driver staring directly at him. The frightened eyes of the other two suspects were also trained on him. He could only watch in frustration as the boat raced away.

"They're running from me," said Pirtle into his radio. "They're heading upstream."

Imsdahl, who was nearby, acknowledged and headed that way.

Pirtle now tracked the departing boat through his binoculars, and in the faint light of a bit of a moon he saw the two passengers doing something, in rapid motion, near the stern of the boat.

Probably tossing salmon, he concluded. Both he and Imsdahl had noted that the suspects had had two salmon hanging overboard on a rope before they caught the big one.

When Imsdahl arrived, the wardens conferred briefly, and they decided that Pirtle would remain out of sight near the ramp and Imsdahl would search upriver for the boat. Aware of a series of shallow rapids not far upriver, the wardens doubted that the boat could have gone far.

The river upstream from the ramp passed through a wild area local residents referred to as "the Rock Piles." Huge gold dredges that resembled riverboats had heavily mined over a dozen square miles of river bottom during the early nineteen-hundreds, and they had left their "tailings," enormous ridges of gravel and cobblestones, behind them.

Great groves of cottonwood trees and thickets of poison-oak and blackberries now grew among the tailing piles, giving the area a rugged beauty, but there were few good roads along the river. It was slow going for Imsdahl, bouncing and reeling in his patrol vehicle. He had to go some distance out of his way before he finally reached the river again, about a quarter mile upstream from Pirtle.

Sweeping the area with his roof-mounted spotlight, Imsdahl was surprised to see the boat, grounded on a gravel bar. But the suspects were gone. Imsdahl scanned with his binoculars up and downriver. A tall shadow caught his eye upstream along the river.

Focusing on the shadow, he found it to be a great blue heron, one of the three-foot-tall, long-legged, long-beaked, spear-fishing birds that sometimes hunted at night. He watched as it stalked in slow motion the shallow waters at the river's edge, long neck cocked, ready to deliver a lightning jab at some luckless frog or minnow.

Upon seeing no sign of the missing suspects, Imsdahl made a show of leaving, climbing into his vehicle and departing. But he didn't go far. When well out of sight and hearing distance from the boat, he parked the patrol vehicle and walked back. Finding a hidden place to sit, he settled in to wait and to study the remarkable hunting skills of the heron.

Pirtle waited nearly an hour before he noted headlights. Someone had returned to the pickup and boat trailer. Pirtle alerted Imsdahl and watched as the vehicle started his way. He fired his engine and waited. At the last instant before the pickup's driver would have spotted him, Pirtle pulled out in front of him and snapped on all his lights, including his bright red emergency lights. The pickup lurched to a stop.

Pirtle directed his roof-mounted spotlight inside the pickup's cab revealing its lone occupant, the driver, a look of terror on his face. Pirtle then slipped out, flashlight in his left hand, right hand on the grips of his holstered sidearm. Training his flashlight beam inside the cab, he cautiously approached the driver's window, circling wide to come up from behind.

"STATE GAME WARDEN, SIR! PUT YOUR HANDS UP WHERE I CAN SEE THEM, PLEASE ... THANK YOU!"

Pirtle now leaned close to the open window and searched the pickup's interior with his light. *No weapons in sight.*

"What's the trouble, officer?" said the man, his voice quavering.

"I need to talk to you," said Pirtle, recognizing the man as the suspect who had netted the big salmon. "I need to know why you and your friends ran from me."

"What do you mean?" said the man. "I've never seen you before."

"Would you step out please?" said Pirtle. The man complied. "Now I need you to walk up front and stand in the headlights." Again the man complied. Pirtle took another look inside the pickup, then approached the suspect.

"I saw you in the boat. So, why did you guys drive the boat to the ramp, then back away and run when you saw me?"

"We were going upriver to camp," said the suspect. "But the boat broke down."

"Then I should find a boatload of camping gear, right?" said Pirtle.

"Well ... uh ... ."

"Sir, I'm placing you under arrest," said Pirtle. "Please turn around and put your hands behind your back." In seconds the man was wearing a set of handcuffs and thinking perhaps he needed a change of strategy.

"Okay, okay," he said. "I'm sorry I lied to you. I'll tell you everything."

"Then you can start by telling me where your friends are," said Pirtle.

"Take me back to the boat and I'll call them in."

Pirtle loaded the man into the patrol vehicle, and five bumping and jouncing minutes later, they were with Imsdahl. Nobody had returned to the boat.

"JOHN! . . . LARRY!" the man shouted into the darkness. No answer. "JOHN! . . . LARRY . . . COME ON OUT!" he shouted, but to no avail.

Pirtle now examined the man's fishing and driver's licenses, identifying him as Daniel Jason Bromley. Then as Imsdahl read Bromley his rights from a Miranda warning card, Pirtle ran him through dispatch for outstanding arrest warrants. There were none.

Despite his right to silence, Bromley then grew talkative and told a long, rambling tale.

"Me and my friends fished almost all day today, and we caught lots of salmon, all snagged, so we threw 'em all back. Some guys told us that there were always wardens around and it cost lots of money if you got caught. But then John caught a big one and got greedy. He decided to keep it, even though it was snagged."

"Was that the one that was about 45 pounds?" asked Pirtle. "The one that was hooked behind the dorsal fin?"

"That's the one," said Bromley, somewhat surprised. "It weighed *exactly* 45 pounds. Anyway, it was John driving the boat when we came into the ramp. When he saw you he panicked."

"Did you hear me yelling at you and telling you to come back?" Pirtle asked.

"We heard you, but John wanted to drive upstream a ways and discuss our options."

"What's John's last name?" Pirtle asked.

Bromley was reluctant, but finally said, "It's Costa. John Costa, and Larry's his son. Larry's been in some trouble, and John really didn't want him to get into trouble with the wardens."

"Where are they now?" Pirtle asked.

"Beats me. They were sitting right here when I left."

"Okay," said Pirtle. "How many salmon did you have in the boat?"

"Each of us kept one fish."

"Where are those fish now?" Pirtle asked.

"The last time I saw them they were on the bank, about 30 feet from the boat."

The wardens then conferred briefly, and they decided that they needed to interrogate the missing two suspects before they could decide what violations Bromley should be charged with. Pirtle reached for his radio and asked dispatch to see if a Highway Patrol helicopter was available. Not long thereafter, he was advised that one was on the way.

When the helicopter arrived, it searched the entire area, searchlight ablaze, for over 20 minutes. But to no avail. The missing suspects remained missing.

Pirtle removed Bromley's handcuffs and explained to him that because he had finally been cooperative, he would be going home that night instead of to jail. Charges would be filed against him later. But he was to contact John and Larry Costa as soon as possible and have them phone Pirtle.

"If they don't call us, we'll be coming after them," said Pirtle. Bromley nodded his understanding, and the wardens left him there.

***

At 4:30 the next morning, the duty desk clerk at the Sleepy Inn Motel in Oroville, a good five miles through rough country from the Feather River Outlet Hole, was roused from sleep by two scratched and dirty, exhausted-looking men asking for a room. The older of the two slapped a driver's license and a Visa card on the counter.

"Where's your car?" the clerk inquired in heavily accented English.

"We don't have no car," said the man, his tired eyes appearing neither friendly nor patient. The clerk met his gaze only briefly, then gave him a room.

***

The morning following the salmon case found Pirtle on his way to Dobbins to investigate the CalTIP turkey violation report that had come in the day before. With him was Fish and Game Patrol Lt. Kent Harrison. As they drove, they discussed the situation, all too aware that the case was cold and they had little to go on. But fortune decided to smile upon them.

Programmed into the scanning feature of Pirtle's patrol vehicle radio was the operating frequency of the Yuba County Sheriff's Office. The wardens heard a call that went out over that frequency, and they were surprised to hear of an incident unfolding at an elementary school in Dobbins. A tall, skinny man carrying a rifle had been seen near the school. The result was instant panic, and the school had gone on immediate lockdown.

"Sounds like our man," said Pirtle.

Soon thereafter, they met with Yuba County Deputy Kai Jahnsen. Pirtle explained the reported illegal killing of a wild turkey by a tall, slender, scruffy-looking man with a rifle.

Jahnsen knew of such a man, a troublesome character by the name of Jason Robert Hook.

"I need to talk to him, too," said Jahnsen. "You can follow me there." The wardens then followed Jahnsen to a junky-looking trailer near the outskirts of Dobbins.

Pirtle had been thinking about what to do at the suspect's residence. He knew that the suspect could simply deny everything, and the wardens couldn't touch him. So, Pirtle had devised a plan.

Upon arriving at Hook's trailer, Jahnsen stood back and watched the wardens work. He noted that Pirtle had parked the patrol vehicle immediately in front of the trailer. He was then surprised to see Pirtle step out of his vehicle with some kind of electronic gizmo with an antenna on it. He would later learn that it was a radio tracking device of the kind used by biologists to locate and monitor radio-collared animals.

Pirtle carried the tracking box well away from Hook's trailer. Hook had by now noted the arrival of the wardens and he emerged from his trailer to see what they were up to. When Hook reached Pirtle, the warden was slowly turning in a circle, the tracking box's arrow-shaped antenna thrust out in front of him as though scanning the horizon.

The tracking box was emitting a sound, a rhythmic beep . . . beep . . . beep. At first, Pirtle was pointing the antenna away from Hook's trailer, and the beeping was faint, but as he pointed the antenna more and more toward Hook's trailer, the volume of the beeping increased. When the antenna was pointed directly at Hook's trailer the beeping was at its loudest, then it trailed away as Pirtle moved the antenna beyond the trailer.

"What are you doing here?" said Hook.

Pirtle turned back with the antenna until it was trained on the trailer, and the beeping was again at its loudest.

"Well sir, we're conducting a wild turkey study. We have radio transmitters on some of the turkeys around here. And it looks like you have one of them in your trailer."

"What?" said Hook, suddenly looking nervous.

"Here, look at this," said Pirtle, training the antenna back and forth past Hook's trailer, and it was obvious, even to Hook, that the beeping was loudest when the antenna was pointing directly at the trailer. It was evidence Hook could neither ignore nor explain.

"You must have shot a turkey, huh?" said Pirtle. "We need the transmitter back."

"Well . . . uh . . . I already ate the turkey," said Hook.

"So where's the head and feathers?" Pirtle asked.

"They're around back," said Hook, and the wardens soon had all the evidence they needed to convict the man on a variety of charges. He even brought out his .22 rifle when Pirtle asked for it.

"It's taken you guys a long time to catch me," said Hook, as Pirtle wrote the citation. "A warden wrote me up for fishing in a closed stream one time, and it cost me $150. Since then, I've always killed deer or turkeys or anything else anytime I wanted to, just to get even."

"I see," said Pirtle. "I'll need your signature right here, Mr. Hook." Hook was grumbling to himself as he signed his name and received his copy of the citation. He then walked back to his trailer.

When Hook was gone, Jahnsen approached Pirtle and said, "How did you do that? How did you make that whizbang chirp loudest when it was pointed at the trailer? I never saw a transmitter in those turkey feathers."

"That's because there wasn't one," said Pirtle with a grin. "Here, look."

Pirtle opened the door of his patrol vehicle and pointed to an object on the seat. It was a dog collar, but it was equipped with a radio transmitter and a tiny antenna.

"You'll notice I parked directly in front of the trailer, right?" said Pirtle. "Well, I turned on this radio collar when I got out."

Jahnsen thought about it for a second, then roared with laughter. "You guys are too much."

***

That afternoon, Pirtle was back in Butte County, he and Imsdahl sitting at an interview table at Gridley Police Department across from John Costa, one of the missing salmon snaggers. The man had reluctantly called Pirtle and had agreed to meet with the wardens.

Costa looked terrible. There were ugly scratches on all exposed skin, and his face and arms were swollen and covered with angry red welts. It was as though he had been mauled by a wildcat, then attacked by bees. But Pirtle knew exactly what had happened, and he could envision this man and his grown son fleeing through the darkness in the Rock Piles, diving into blackberry patches to elude a searching helicopter.

Costa told his story about running from the wardens, and the wardens immediately knew that it was largely fictional. For Costa had been driving the boat when it backed away from the ramp, and Costa was now claiming that Bromley was responsible.

"Wait a minute," said Pirtle. "You're saying that Bromley grabbed the wheel and was controlling the boat?"

"That's right," said Costa. "I didn't want to run from you."

Imsdahl then threw in a question. "So, Bromley must have reached over you and grabbed the gear shift and throttle as well?"

"Uh . . . well . . . I guess so."

And so it went. The wardens' hopes of extracting a clean confession from Costa were dashed. The man was obviously throwing his friend Bromley to the dogs, just as Bromley had cheerfully given up Costa's name. Each was blaming the other for everything. But the wardens had enough evidence from their own observations to charge Bromley and John Costa with a variety of crimes.

When the interview was over, Pirtle again studied Costa's inflamed and swollen face and arms, and he was reminded that justice was sometimes swift in coming.

"It looks like you must have run through a little poison-oak the other night," said Pirtle.

"No," said Costa grimly, peering at Pirtle through eyes that had been reduced by swelling to mere slits. "We ran through a *lot* of poison-oak."

The Worst of the Worst

The tiny plane was but a speck in the vast and moonless night sky, its single engine all but inaudible to the few sleepless souls who at 3:00 a.m. might have listened for it.

The plane's sole occupant was Lt. James Halber, California Department of Fish and Game. Looking down from 10,000 feet above the Sierra Nevada foothills, he could see the lights of a single pickup truck meandering along a remote dirt road behind locked gates. The intensity of Halber's scrutiny was not unlike that of a coyote regarding a quail.

Halber throttled back and put the plane into a slight bank, settling into a 10-mile-diameter overhead circle around the pickup, the occupants of which were attempting to poach deer in the oak and Digger pine forest. Someone in the pickup was operating a powerful spotlight, directing it right and left, sweeping the bright beam over the countryside, almost certainly searching for the big bucks that inhabited the area. Other wardens Halber had radioed just minutes earlier were racing to the area to make the arrests.

Two hours later, on a remote and winding road, two wardens in a green patrol rig made a highly hazardous head-on stop of the pickup. The two vehicles abruptly stopped, 20 feet between their front bumpers, and the wardens leaped out and hurried forward, flashlights in hand. The two suspects in the pickup, half blinded by a powerful roof-mounted spotlight on the patrol rig, had their hands up to shield their eyes.

Within eight seconds of the stop, there was a warden peering into each of the side windows of the pickup, further illuminating the unshaven, villainous-looking men within. But despite the fact that such suspects are almost always heavily armed, the wardens' careful search of the vehicle revealed neither firearms nor archery gear. And neither suspect had seemed particularly surprised when they were stopped.

"We're just out for a drive," said one of the two suspects, an insolent grin on his face.

Halber, still circling above, was highly annoyed. He had intentionally delayed the stop until the suspects were miles from the area in which they had been hunting, a measure intended to defeat poachers who stash their weapons and make "dry runs" out of the area to draw out any wardens lurking about.

The wardens had no choice but to release the suspects, and Halber found it a particularly bitter pill to swallow. He had tangled with one of them several times before. Victor Prague was a habitual violator, one of the worst. Despite the fact that Halber had arrested him and seen him convicted at least three times in years past, the man not only continued to violate, but he was always arrogant, obnoxious and verbally abusive to the wardens.

But the other suspect released by the wardens that night was something else. Rumors abounded that Martin Mattos, a convicted felon who could not legally possess firearms, was even more committed to poaching game than his friend Prague. The difference, however, was that Mattos was both smart and clever, and he always had a plan to thwart the wardens. Despite over 20 years of poaching, he had never been caught.

And so it was on this night. What was undoubtedly Mattos' plan had worked perfectly. He and Prague had spent a night spotlighting and had probably killed a deer. But despite the fact that they had been observed from the air by Halber, they had evaded arrest and prosecution. Had they not been stopped by the wardens, they would have returned the following day for the stashed guns and the deer when there was far less chance of encountering wardens.

Halber knew then that it would take another night and skillful work by the wardens to catch Mattos. But for Halber, there would be no other night, for a few months later he retired from the profession he loved after over 30 years of service. His failure to catch Mattos was just one of many bits of unfinished business, heavy on his heart, that would never be resolved.

Or would it?

***

Two years later.

It was just after dark when a small moving-and-storage van rolled into a seedy neighborhood of Oroville and stopped on a potholed street littered with all manner of junk and broken-down vehicles. Every house was in danger of collapse, pit bulls ran loose and ragged kids raced around on dirt bikes.

The driver of the van was a stubble-faced, disheveled-looking man, who looked as though he would have been at home pushing his belongings in a shopping cart. He stepped out and hurried away as though on a mission. A dozen sets of suspicious eyes peering from doors and windows watched him go.

But things aren't always what they seem. The untidy man walked a half mile to a better part of town and climbed into an unremarkable-looking pickup truck. Reaching beneath the seat, he grabbed the microphone of a hidden radio and spoke into it.

"You're on your own, Josh," he said. Then he started the engine and drove away.

Back at the parked moving van, Fish and Game Warden Josh Brennan, padlocked inside the cavernous rear storage compartment, peered out through a slit in the wall. The focus of his attention was a dilapidated house across the street, the residence of Martin Mattos, who he had come to regard as perhaps the most destructive game poacher in Butte County.

Brennan's opinion of Mattos was borne of two unpleasant encounters with Mattos and another scoundrel, Victor Prague, the previous deer season. Brennan and another warden, Matt Galli, had observed them spotlighting from their pickup one dark night, but when the wardens stopped them, they had no weapons. The frustrated wardens thoroughly searched their vehicle, a green extended-cab pickup, but found nothing. They searched the engine compartment and Galli even crawled under the vehicle and searched the undercarriage. All the while the suspects laughed at them and chided them.

A few weeks later, on another dark night, Brennan blundered onto the two men standing on a road near Lake Oroville, having obviously been dropped off by someone. They were armed with rifles, powerful hand-held lights, and they had a single walkie-talkie radio with them, its switch in the *On* position.

When Brennan asked them where their vehicle was, Prague, verbally abusive as always and with a permanent smirk on his face, said they had lost their pickup in the lake when the emergency brake failed. The two men had then separated, one attempting to get behind Brennan, testing him. Brennan retreated a few feet, hand on his gun, and Prague spoke again.

"We're gonna find you out here someday without your badge, and we'll see how tough you are then."

Brennan felt threatened enough that he keyed his mike and called for a backup, something he almost never did. Wardens raced from several directions, emergency lights ablaze, sirens blaring. And there had been enough urgency in Brennan's voice that an armed U.S. Forest Service agent and a Butte County deputy responded as well.

The first of the backup units arrived surprisingly quickly, and the suspects immediately became polite and cooperative. Unfortunately, Brennan had not seen them break any laws, and ultimately they were released.

Later that night Brennan met with Galli and the other backup wardens at a coffee shop in Oroville to discuss the incident. All were in agreement that Mattos and Prague were careful and clever poachers, and they were using others to assist them, to act as lookouts or to drop them off. It was a genuine poaching ring, well-organized and apparently of the belief that they were uncatchable.

That night Brennan and Galli made the decision to devote the next deer season to doing whatever it took to catch Mattos and Prague and the others, to put an end to their crimes against wildlife. What it would take, the wardens knew, was time. Lots of time. They therefore devised a plan of war to attack the poachers where they were most vulnerable. They would undertake an extended stakeout of the suspects' homes.

Months later, as deer season approached, Brennan and Galli began shadowing the suspects, gathering information, learning their work habits and how they spent their days.

It soon became apparent that Mattos, if he had an honest job, worked odd and unusual hours. He had a flatbed car-hauler trailer he parked in front of his house, and he would leave with it empty, often after dark, and return with it empty before dawn. Because he had done time for vehicle theft, the wardens thought it likely he was engaged in it again, for he had no other apparent means of support. Prague, the wardens learned, was a truck driver, often driving for 12 hours or more a day

When deer season opened, the wardens began their stakeout in earnest, putting into play their plan using the moving van and an undercover pickup. They took turns in the moving van, alternating nights, and each morning one of them would walk in and drive the moving van out with the other still locked inside. And so it went, night after night, and their plan soon began to pay off.

But there were problems at first. A strong criminal element in the neighborhood was nervous over the appearance in their midst of a vehicle that could contain enemies of one sort or another. There were times when people would bang on the side of the van, put their ears against it to listen or shout things like, "We know you're in there. We're gonna call the cops."

One time a small crowd gathered on either side of the van and rocked it violently from side to side. Brennan's main fear was that they would set the van on fire; locked inside, he could only remain very still and ride it out. But as days passed, the local residents became more accustomed to the van and more or less left it alone.

One of the first things that became evident when the wardens began the stakeout was that the residence next door to Mattos' housed a drug dealer. On Friday and Saturday nights, a procession of vehicles would come and go. People would drive up, go inside for a minute or two, then leave.

One night, Brennan was on watch in the moving van, and he saw a man drive up, park in front, then go to the door. Seconds after he disappeared inside, the door flew open and the same man bolted out at a full sprint, closely pursued by five other men. His pursuers caught him near his vehicle and savagely kicked and beat him into unconsciousness, leaving him lying motionless in the dirt just a few feet from Brennan.

Brennan wrestled briefly with the moral dilemma of what to do about drug dealers beating up drug dealers. But then the victim began showing signs of life, groaning and moving his head from side to side. Finally he sat up, looked around, struggled to his feet, limped to his car and drove away.

As for evidence of poaching activity, it was apparent from the first. Almost every night, Prague and two other men would arrive at Mattos' house at around 10 p.m. in Prague's green extended-cab pickup. They would go inside for a few minutes, then emerge with Mattos. At various times they tested super-bright spotlights in front of the house or toyed with a hand-held scanner the wardens would later learn was tuned to Fish and Game's radio frequency. Then they would all climb into the pickup.

But each night before they drove away, Mattos' wife would come out of the house with a long object wrapped in a blanket. Because Mattos was a felon, the wardens were certain the long object was a rifle. Mrs. Mattos would hand the object to someone inside the pickup, then the truckload of poachers would depart.

Whichever warden was not in the moving van would tail the suspects, and the wardens soon learned that the poachers were creatures of habit. Upon leaving Mattos' house, they would drive to the same gas station each night and buy gas. Then they would head out of town toward their favorite hunting grounds.

As night after night passed, the wardens began to get lucky. One morning, just at dawn, Brennan watched the suspects return with the antlers of a large buck visible above the pickup bed, a buck that could not have been legally taken. It had to have been taken at night, a clear violation of state law.

A few nights later, Galli peered from the van as the suspects returned home, again just at dawn, but this time with the antlers of two huge bucks visible in the back. Later that day, the wardens tailed the suspects as they drove around town with the big bucks, showing their friends and anyone else who cared to look.

At one point, the pickup with the bucks was parked at the home of Samuel Perez, whom the wardens had identified as one of the two lesser members of the poaching ring. Because the wardens were curious to know if the two bucks were tagged, they enlisted the help of the sheriff's office.

Soon a sheriff's office unit cruised by Perez's house, as though on a call, and the officers got a peek inside the green pickup. The deputy then surprised the wardens by informing them that there were not just two bucks in the pickup, but three, all apparently tagged. That afternoon, the wardens tailed the suspects to Prague's residence and watched as the three bucks were dumped in a side yard next to the house. But now the tags had been removed.

But the real break for the wardens came a night or two later when Mrs. Mattos was careless bringing a rifle from the house out to the pickup when her husband and the others were ready to head out. The blanket concealing the rifle fell open and Galli clearly saw the weapon.

This was bad news for Mattos, for as a convicted felon, forbidden to possess firearms in his home or anywhere else, the presence of a rifle in his house could be enough to send him back to prison. But it certainly provided the wardens with probable cause for a search warrant of the Mattos residence, a search that would surely provide them with other incriminating evidence against their main suspect.

Because Mattos was as good as in the bag, the wardens now concentrated their efforts on Prague, the number two man. Because they couldn't use the moving van at Prague's residence, which was in a more rural neighborhood on the other side of town, the wardens had to travel on foot to get in close.

In order to better observe Prague's house, the wardens chose separate locations from which to watch from two different vantage points in grass and shrubbery. Not long after they were in place, Galli, who had made a nest in high grass, was startled to hear a deep, guttural grunting sound coming his way. Soon thereafter, Brennan was surprised to get a text message from Galli that read, "Dude, there's a giant pig out here."

It was true. Several hundred pounds of pork, on the hoof and curious, had come to investigate. It apparently had the run of the neighborhood. But it proved harmless, and after giving Galli a good sniffing, it lost interest and ambled away.

On another night, while the suspects were out poaching, Brennan received a phone call from an informant who lived in a remote place in the area where the suspects hunted. The informant reported hearing a shot down the road and seeing a large green pickup there.

"We know who they are," said Brennan. "We're watching them. Stay away from them and let them do what they're going to do."

But the informant couldn't contain himself. He just had to go and shout to the suspects that he had called the wardens. The suspects immediately fled.

Highly annoyed at the informant, Brennan and Galli drove to the location the following day. They searched the area and found a large buck that had been shot the night before, its eyes still bright and clear. Suspecting that the suspects might still return at least for the large antlers, Brennan knelt beside the buck and with his knife carved a tiny X on the base of its right antler. The wardens then departed.

That night, the informant called Brennan again and said that he thought the suspects had returned and dropped someone off. The following day the wardens again went to the place and found that the head and antlers of the buck were missing, which was exactly what they had hoped for.

It was becoming more and more apparent to the wardens that the highly organized poaching activity they had been observing constituted a criminal conspiracy on the part of the four suspects. It was clear that they were conspiring to break the law, which was a serious thing. Poaching deer was a misdemeanor, but criminal conspiracy was a felony.

With this in mind, Brennan approached Mike Ramsey, Butte County's hard-nosed district attorney, and filled him in on what was going on.

"They do it almost every night, Mike," said Brennan. "And they've been doing it for years."

Ramsey, whose father had once been a game warden, was in agreement. Even in a rural county where a slight bending of Fish and Game laws now and then was socially acceptable to many, Mattos and his friends were way over the line. They needed to be stopped and taught a lesson.

Ramsey advised Brennan to get to work immediately on a search warrant for Mattos' residence, explaining that while Galli's observation of the rifle coming out of the house was good probable cause for the moment, it would be weakened with the passage of time.

"You have about 10 days," said Ramsey, which meant to Brennan that he and Galli had but a few remaining days to gather enough probable cause for search warrants for the homes of Prague and the two lesser suspects. And Brennan and Galli were willing to settle for nothing less.

As it turned out, they had already made enough observations of incriminating things to allow them to go for search warrants for the homes of the other suspects. At the very least they had documented all four suspects on two separate occasions leaving after dark and returning at first light with deer that had to have been spotlighted during the night. So the wardens now began the task of writing the necessary reports and affidavits and planning a grand takedown.

The grand takedown involved 15 wardens divided into three teams of five. They were to hit the homes of Mattos, Prague and Perez simultaneously. The fourth suspect, they had learned, lived with Prague.

It was late one morning when four Fish and Game patrol rigs turned onto the potholed road Brennan and Galli had come to know so well. One peeled off and took an alley to the rear of Mattos' house. The others slid to stops in front and four uniformed wardens leaped out. It was Brennan who pounded on the front door.

"STATE GAME WARDENS! WE HAVE A SEARCH WARRANT! OPEN UP!"

Mattos opened the door looking as though he was facing the gallows.

"Mr. Mattos!" said Brennan in greeting. "Turn around and put your hands behind your back." Mattos, as though in a daze, complied and Brennan handcuffed him. Brennan then sat him down in a recliner and cautioned him to stay there.

The search of Mattos' house revealed numerous things of interest to the wardens. There were hundreds of photos of Mattos and the other suspects with trophy bucks, photos that went back 15 years or more. The wardens located the hand-held scanner and confirmed that it was tuned to Fish and Game's frequency, and they located a selection of powerful 12-volt spotlights. Hanging on rafters in the garage, they were amazed to see the antlers of over 100 big bucks.

Most interesting, however, was the grisly sight that awaited the wardens when they inspected the back yard. There, placed on objects around the yard, they found the severed heads and massive antlers of five trophy-sized bucks.

But the wardens found no guns, their primary objective for the search. Puzzled and disappointed, Brennan took another walk through the house, and it was then that his attention was drawn to a stepladder leaning against the wall in a hallway. Looking up at the ceiling he spotted a carefully concealed opening, a crawl-hole into the attic.

By then, Mattos' wife had been allowed to join him where he was under guard by a warden, and she was there when Brennan set up the stepladder and asked young Warden Byron

Hernandez to climb up and investigate. Hernandez climbed the ladder, pushed the door open and hoisted himself into the attic.

For a few seconds there was silence, then Brennan called up to Hernandez and asked him what he could see.

"Guns," said Hernandez. "I see guns."

It was then that Mattos spoke to his wife in an elevated voice intended to be heard by the wardens.

"I've never been up in that attic. Have you?"

"No, not me," came his wife's reply. "I've never been up there."

The wardens found this exchange amusing and laughed as Hernandez handed down two scoped rifles and a shotgun.

Meanwhile, Galli and his team had hit Prague's house, finding him away at work. Forcing open a door, they went in to conduct their search. They found a freezer full of deer meat, a few sets of deer antlers and various other bits of minor evidence.

At the third residence being searched that morning, that of Samuel Perez, the wardens recovered an illegally taken and untagged bear, plus a large amount of frozen deer meat. They also recovered a fresh set of untagged deer antlers.

"I didn't shoot that deer," cried Perez. "I found it dead with an arrow in it, and I just wanted the antlers."

One of the wardens then pointed out the tiny X that Brennan had carved near the base of the right antler. Perez appeared thoroughly deflated.

Back at Mattos' residence, the wardens were gathering evidence, preparing to depart. Brennan had informed Mattos that he was going to jail for being a felon in possession of firearms. Brennan had also read Mattos his rights and asked him if he was willing to talk about his crimes.

"I'll make a deal with you," said Mattos. "If you take me out the back door so my kids don't see you taking me away, I'll tell you everything."

Brennan agreed to the deal, and Mattos spoke for several minutes, explaining how, for many years, he and his friends had defeated the wardens.

"We always used lookouts. We would let somebody out with the rifle and radio to hide while we went in to look for a deer with the spotlight. When we spotted a good buck, we would drive back to the lookout, get the rifle and go back and shoot the deer. Then we would drop someone off with the deer and stash the rifle. We got stopped lots of times by wardens, but we never had a deer or a rifle with us. That's how we beat you. We would pick up the deer only after it was tagged and we were sure there were no wardens around."

Brennan listened, totally engrossed, and then asked lots of questions. Mattos answered them all. Brennan then took him out the back door to a waiting patrol rig and took him to jail where he was booked on felony charges. Arrest warrants were later issued for Prague and Perez, but they turned themselves in before the wardens could get to them.

The cases never went to trial. Ramsey had appointed Deputy District Attorney Kurt Worley to prosecute the case, and Worley, when the time came, was totally prepared, knowing the 200-page arrest report inside and out. It was clear to the defense attorneys that they were facing a fight they wouldn't win, so they convinced their clients to change their pleas to guilty, which they did.

All of them were convicted of criminal conspiracy, a felony, plus they were convicted for numerous Fish and Game violations. All were sentenced to several months in jail, their rifles and equipment ordered destroyed, and they were fined thousands of dollars.

When it was all over, the wardens, particularly Brennan and Galli, felt good about the case. They had invested a huge amount of time, but it had paid off. They had brought to justice the worst of the worst, perhaps the most destructive wildlife-abusing outlaws in Butte and surrounding counties. They would always remember the case with pride.

They came away with other memories as well, some good and some bad. One particularly outrageous memory would always send them into fits of laughter. It involved the interrogation of suspect Samuel Perez by wardens Sean Pirtle and Brett Gomes.

Perez had denied everything. He stood handcuffed as the wardens first accused him of participating in the killing of the buck Brennan had marked with an X on its antlers.

"I wasn't even with them on that night," he said. "You can't pin that on me."

Gomes then pulled out a photo Galli had taken while concealed in the moving van. It clearly showed Perez, holding a rifle in front of Mattos' house with Mattos and Prague. Gomes showed the photo to Perez, who started to shake. Then his knees buckled and he collapsed to a sitting position on his couch.

He sat on the couch hyperventilating for a few seconds, then he began to sob, tears streaming down his face. It soon became apparent to the embarrassed wardens that the man desperately needed to blow his nose. But he even more desperately needed something else.

"I need a chew, man," Perez sobbed. "I really need a chew."

Gomes, looking on, felt pity for the man and located a can of Copenhagen. Popping off the lid, he held the can in front of Perez's face. Perez immediately buried his face in the can, rooting around until he emerged with his lower lip stuffed full and his face hideously smeared with a mixture of tears, snot and chewing tobacco.

Pirtle stared at him for a second or two, disgusted, then glanced around the room and said, "We need something to wipe his face."

"It's okay," said Perez, who then bent down and wiped his face on the arm of his couch.

MASTERS OF DECEPTION

The first bright rays of morning sunlight were just appearing above Sawmill Peak as a Fish and Game patrol vehicle crept along an abandoned logging spur. At the wheel, Warden Josh Brennan scanned not only the road ahead, but the sky above it.

Then movement caught his eye. A dozen or so band-tailed pigeons came rocketing over the ridge, made a sweeping descending circle, then slowed to flutter down into the upper branches of a dead oak tree. Brennan stopped the patrol rig, turned off the engine and listened. The strange, owl-like calls of the band-tails were clearly audible in the still morning air, a wild sound that never failed to delight Brennan.

The band-tails looked and acted much like mourning doves, but they were considerably larger and more colorful. Not only did they have yellow legs and bills, but they had broad patches of iridescent greenish-bronze feathers on their backs below white crescents on their necks. And of course there was the wide band of light gray on their tail feathers that had inspired their name.

A bit of sadness crept over Brennan as he peered at the band-tails through his binoculars, for they were becoming fewer. This was true at least in the places he was used to seeing them. Where he had once seen hundreds, he now saw mere dozens.

Brennan started the engine and continued on his way. He had not gone far, however, when he encountered something else that brought him to an immediate halt. The ground along one side of the road was covered with band-tail feathers, piles of them, as though 20 or more of the birds had been plucked there. And empty shotgun shells were everywhere. Brennan stepped out and picked up one of the shot-shell empties and sniffed it. The stench of fired powder was still detectable in it, no more than a few days old.

More pigeons now arrived, many of them passing well within shotgun range of Brennan. Band-tailed pigeons were still hunted in California, but the hunting season for band-tails was still a week away. Someone had started early, ignoring state law.

After carefully studying the ground at the kill site, Brennan began picking up the empty shotgun shells and placing them into a plastic ziplock bag. Then he took a sample of the pigeon feathers and placed them in a second ziplock bag. He was about to leave when he noticed something else. Here and there near the feathers were a number of cigarette butts, smoked down to mere nubs. Brennan collected these as well, placing them in a labeled evidence bag.

Brennan did all of these things despite the fact that his chances for coming up with a suspect or suspects for this wildlife crime were poor at best. He did these things because that's what good investigators did, and Brennan had a history of making long-shots pay off.

Upon returning home that night, Brennan phoned his supervisor and made an unusual request.

"I need about a hundred bucks to buy cigarettes," he said.

"You need what?" came his lieutenant's bewildered reply.

The following day, Brennan entered a cut-rate cigarette store in Chico and bought one pack each of every brand of cigarettes the store carried. He then returned to his home and photographed a cigarette of each brand beside the pack in which it came and a small ruler for size reference. He compiled all of the photos onto a CD and made copies of it. Having created a data base for the brand identification of cigarette butts, Brennan now distributed copies of it for reference by other wardens.

During the course of this project, Brennan was able to identify the brand of the cigarette butts he had recovered among the pigeon feathers. They were *Newport* brand, *Full Flavor*, a bit of information that could at some future time provide supportive evidence against a violator who smoked the same brand. With this done, he filed everything away to await some new development that might help him piece together a case. As it happened, he didn't have long to wait. The call came the following day.

"Someone's shooting band-tails out of season," said the caller. "I went up this morning to scout out a place to hunt this weekend, and I found where someone had already shot a bunch of 'em."

"You mean up on Sawmill Peak?" Brennan asked. "I already know about it."

The caller paused, then said, "Then you know about the bear?"

"Bear?" Brennan inquired.

"Yes. There's a dead bear up there in a little meadow a short way past the feathers. Someone cut one hindquarter off and left the rest."

Brennan questioned the caller further about the location of the dead bear, then thanked him for the information. Within minutes he was in his patrol rig, headed for Sawmill Peak. When he reached the pile of feathers, where he had turned around the day before, he continued on and located the meadow.

Brennan smelled the stench of death long before he spotted the carcass of the bear. As he approached it, his stomach turned. His intention had been to dig a bullet from the carcass, a revolting task he had done a number of times on a number of rotting carcasses. But this one was in the absolute worst stage of decomposition, a seething mass of maggots.

Spotting a large wound on the animal's neck, he attempted to cut into it, but he retched and gagged violently, nearly vomiting, and had to give up. But he would try again another day, when the maggots had finished their work.

Brennan now had an out-of-season bear case to go with the out-of-season pigeon case. Were the same bad guys responsible for both? Most likely, Brennan concluded. But it would take good luck to come up with suspects.

***

About the time Brennan was retching over the dead bear, TV dish-installer Rod Bubier, an employee of a local satellite TV company, had just leaned his extension ladder against a new home in the ridgetop community of Paradise. As he climbed the ladder, satellite dish under one arm, he happened to glance over a fence into the tiny back yard of an apartment next door. Something there caught his eye.

Near the back door of the apartment were the naked, plucked carcasses of four birds, two large and two much smaller. Because Bubier was a hunter, he had no trouble identifying the species of the plucked birds. The larger ones had to be wild turkeys, and the smaller ones were obviously pheasants. He also knew that the hunting seasons for both species were not yet open.

Bubier finished with the job, returned to his truck and phoned Fish and Game. A dispatcher took the call and soon had him connected to Brennan, who took the report with great interest. When Brennan had gleaned all pertinent information from Bubier, he thanked the man.

"I'll let you know what happens," said Brennan, and he meant it.

A half hour later, he pulled up in front of the apartment in Paradise. As he approached the front door, he spotted what appeared to be three large animal teeth on the concrete step. Taking a closer look, he recognized them to be the freshly extracted canine "fangs" of an adult bear. Flesh was still attached to the teeth, and it appeared they had been laid there to dry. Brennan immediately thought of the dead bear near Sawmill Peak.

Brennan pulled a handkerchief from his pocket, wrapped the teeth in it and stuffed the small bundle into his pocket. He then knocked on the door. The door opened, and Brennan found himself facing a woman, probably in her mid-thirties, who looked strangely familiar.

"Good afternoon, ma'am, I'm . . . ."

"I know who you are," the woman broke in, all smiles. "You're the game warden."

As she spoke, she turned and called to a man of about the same age.

"Hey Billy, guess who's here? It's the game warden. You know, the one we met at that class."

It now dawned on Brennan. A month earlier, he had attended a hunter education class in Chico. These two people, man and wife, had been the only adults among 15 or so young students. They had seemed so out of place. But they had passed the course and received their certificates.

It was immediately apparent to Brennan that Billy was not nearly as happy to see him as was his exuberant wife. Billy, in fact, appeared highly uneasy.

"Hello, again," said Brennan. "Can I come in?" Billy was silent, but the woman responded instantly.

"Sure, come on in. I'm Brenda, remember?"

Brennan entered what was an amazingly small one-bedroom apartment. He refused an invitation to sit, and he got right to the point.

"This isn't a social visit. I need you to tell me about the turkeys and the pheasants you've got."

Both of them suddenly appeared stricken, and it took a few seconds for Billy to find his voice.

"We don't know nothin' about no turkeys or pheasants."

"Well, I got a tip that you killed two turkeys and two pheasants," said Brennan. "Is that true?"

"No, it's not true. We didn't kill nothin'."

"Well, I guess we'd better look in the back yard," said Brennan.

Brenda and Billy looked stricken anew as Brennan made a move toward the sliding glass door to the back yard.

"Wait a minute, wait a minute," said Billy holding up his hands to halt Brennan. "Okay, we did it. You got us. But we killed 'em to eat. I got laid off my job, and Brenda's on disability."

"But I notice you've got plenty of beer and cigarettes," said Brennan, pointing to a case of beer by the refrigerator and two cartons of cigarettes on a table. "So you can't be too hard up."

Brennan questioned them thoroughly and learned that they had shot the turkeys crossing a road near the Feather River and had shot the two pheasants in the Sacramento Valley near Richvale. Brennan then had them take him out to the tiny back yard.

Upon seeing the back yard for the first time, Brennan was taken aback by the piles of accumulated trash and garbage there. Seeing his reaction, Brenda explained.

"I don't want you to think we're slobs or anything, but we're being evicted, and that's where we put our trash." If there was logic to this explanation it was lost on Brennan.

The four plucked birds were there, just as Bubier had said they would be. Brennan labeled each with evidence tags.

"Now you need to tell me about the band-tailed pigeons," said Brennan.

The two glanced at one another, wide eyed and again panic stricken, as though finding themselves in the presence of a mind reader. Again it was Billy who first found his voice.

"Pigeons? What do you mean pigeons? We don't know nothin' about no pigeons."

"Well," said Brennan. "We found the big pile of pigeon feathers, and we found the 12 gage empties you left there. And guess what else we found?"

"What else?" said the two of them in unison.

"We found cigarette butts. Lots of them. All the same Brand . . . Newports . . . Newport Full Flavor. What brand of cigarettes do you two smoke?" As he spoke, Brennan looked over at the cartons of Newport Full Flavor cigarettes on the table.

"That don't mean nothin'," said Billy. "Lots of people smoke Newports."

"Yeah, lots of people," echoed Brenda.

"True, but these have your DNA on them. Now, you need to know that DNA testing is very expensive, and if the tests prove those butts belonged to you, you may have to pay the expenses. So if those butts were yours, you need to tell me now."

The two looked at one another in anguish, torn by indecision. Brenda started to cry. Finally Billy spoke.

"Okay. We admit it. We shot the pigeons."

"Where are those pigeons now?" Brennan asked.

"We ate 'em," said Billy. "We ate every one of 'em."

"Okay," said Brennan. "Now I need for you to tell me about the bear."

More panic. More wide-eyed looking at each other. Finally Billy spoke.

"Bear? What bear? We don't know nothin' about no bear."

"No," said Brenda. "We don't know nothin'."

"Tell you what," said Brennan. "You need to think about that."

Brennan now asked for and examined their driver's licenses.

"So, it's Mr. and Mrs. Treadwell?"

"That's right," said Billy.

Brennan jotted down their ID information and explained to them that he intended to file charges against the two of them through the district attorney's office. With this done, he bade them a temporary farewell.

"I'm going now, but I'll be back," he said.

He packed the evidence birds out to his patrol rig and departed, leaving the Treadwells to brood over his ominous promise.

True to his word, Brennan was back the following afternoon. Billy Treadwell answered the door and frowned at the sight of him.

"We need to talk some more," said Brennan. "Can I come in?"

Billy reluctantly invited him in. Brenda was not pleased to see him.

"You told me that you didn't know about a bear," said Brennan. "But the evidence shows that you were there when the bear was there. How could you not know about it?"

Billy thought furiously, but despite the fact that a good liar could have easily provided a number of reasonable explanations to satisfy this question, Billy could come up with nothing. He looked to Brenda for inspiration, but she returned only a blank stare.

"Okay, okay," Billy finally blurted out. "We saw the bear there, but we didn't shoot it."

"No," said Brenda. "We didn't shoot it."

"Did you touch the bear or do anything with it?" Brennan asked.

"No," said Billy. "We didn't touch it."

Brennan now pulled from his pocket a ziplock sandwich bag containing the three bear teeth.

"Then what about these?" he said, placing the bag on the table.

The Treadwells stared in horror, first at the teeth, then at each other, and finally at Brennan.

"Okay, okay," said Billy. "We cut these teeth and some meat off the bear, but we didn't shoot it."

"What did you do with the meat?" Brennan asked.

"We tried to eat it, but it was terrible," said Billy. "We threw it away."

"But you're telling me that you didn't shoot the bear? You need to tell it to me straight if you did," said Brennan.

"No," said Billy. "We positively did not shoot that bear."

"Positively!" added Brenda.

Brennan now made hard eye contact with both of them for a few seconds.

"I'm going now, but I'll be back. You need to think about this real hard."

Brennan now turned and strode out the door.

He didn't return the following day. He chose instead to let the Treadwells stew for a while longer. But the day after that, he was back again, banging on the front door. He got no answer. He banged louder. No answer.

"I know you're in there," shouted Brennan. "Open up."

Finally the door opened. Brenda peered out and delivered an absolutely ludicrous explanation for why they had not immediately opened the door. Then she invited Brennan in.

Facing Billy, Brennan said, "Did you know there's a warrant out for your arrest in Santa Cruz County?"

Billy blanched white. "I have a warrant?"

"That's right," said Brennan. "That's why it's all the more important for you to tell me the truth, because I have to decide what to do about that warrant. Now, did you shoot that bear?"

Billy squirmed uncomfortably but stuck to his story.

"No," he said emphatically. "We found the dead bear and cut some meat off of it but we didn't shoot it."

"I think you're lying to me," said Brennan. "I'm going to leave now and let you think about this. But I will be back."

Brennan again departed.

Two days later, morning found Brennan back at Sawmill Peak, examining the dead bear. The carcass was dryer now, the hordes of maggots greatly reduced. Brennan held his breath, grabbed the carcass by a front foot, lifted it and gave it a good shake to dislodge more of the maggots. To his surprise, something else fell out.

Brennan dropped the carcass and picked up the object. It was a disk of flattened lead about the size of a fifty-cent piece. He recognized it for what it was, what remained of a 12 gage rifled slug. It made perfect sense. The Treadwells had no rifle, but they both had 12 gage shotguns. So, they had apparently taken rifled slug shells with them to shoot deer or bear if they got the opportunity.

Unfortunately for Brennan, fired rifled shotgun slugs cannot be matched to specific shotguns. But fired shotgun shell casings could indeed be matched through extractor marks to the shotguns that fired them. Brennan, therefore, had to find the fired casing in order to match it to one of the Treadwells' shotguns.

Brennan first did an expanding circle search around the bear, which had died near the center of the one-acre meadow. But he found nothing. He therefore began a search of the dense foliage surrounding the meadow, tangles of poison-oak and other native plants. It was a daunting task, a needle in a haystack search, but Brennan kept at it.

Brennan knew that while the shooter had probably fired from one of many game trails leading to the meadow, the ejected empty casing would probably have landed well off the trail in heavy brush. But he also knew that ejected casings from the Treadwells' shotguns would most likely fly to the right of the game trails as the shooter approached the meadow. So he searched accordingly.

Well over an hour passed before Brennan spotted a tiny splash of red color in a poison-oak bush. He carefully reached in, avoiding the troublesome tri-leafed vegetation as best he could, and withdrew the fired casing of a Winchester 12 gage rifled slug round.

It was toward evening that same day that Brennan again pulled up in front of the home of the husband and wife poaching team. He knocked on the door, and Brenda answered, giving him an unhappy when-are-you-going-to-leave-us-alone look. But she invited him in. He sat opposite them at the small table.

"It's time you told me the truth," said Brennan. "I know you shot that bear."

"No, we didn't," Billy exclaimed. "I told you, we just found it there and cut some meat off of it."

Brennan made hard eye contact with them for a few seconds, then withdrew from his pocket the flattened slug he had recovered from the carcass of the bear. He placed it on the table and slid it across to Billy.

"Do you know what this is?" Brennan asked.

Billy obviously knew exactly what it was but he didn't answer.

"It's time you told me the truth, Mr. Treadwell," said Brennan. "If I have to, I'll send this slug and your shotguns to the lab for ballistics testing. They can match this slug to the rifling in your shotgun barrel."

The fact that shotgun barrels do not have rifling did not occur to either of the Treadwells. They looked at one another, again on the verge of panic.

"Ballistics testing is expensive," Brennan continued. "If it proves you killed the bear, the judge will probably make you pay for the testing. Do you want to take that chance?"

Billy took a series of deep breaths, then replied, "Okay, I shot the bear, but it was self-defense. He was eating our pigeons."

"Eating your pigeons?" said Brennan. "Self-defense?"

"Yeah. Every time we shot a pigeon, the bear would find it and eat it. So we had to shoot him."

"Yeah," said Brenda, nodding her head enthusiastically. "We had to shoot him."

Brennan could only shake his head in wonder as he pondered what was perhaps the dumbest story he had ever heard. But it was an admission to killing the bear. He could have ended his investigation at this point. He had enough to convict them in court. But there was something in him that demanded to know the real motive for the violation and exactly how events went down.

"When are you going to tell it to me straight?" said Brennan. "That story you just told me may have just earned you a ride to Santa Cruz in handcuffs."

"But that's what happened," said Billy, bristling. "I'll fight you in court."

"Last chance, Mr. Treadwell," said Brennan earnestly. "You have a lot to lose here."

Billy looked at Brenda again for possible guidance, but again his wife was absolutely no help. He got up and paced back and forth in the tiny kitchen, torn by indecision. Finally he turned to Brennan.

"If I tell it to you straight, will you forget about taking me to jail?"

"I won't take you to jail," said Brennan. "But I need to hear the real truth."

Okay, okay," said Billy. "I shot a pigeon and when I went to get it, I saw the bear. I thought he was gonna attack me, so I shot him."

"Let me get this straight," said Brennan. "You were shooting pigeons with bird-shot, you saw a bear and thought he was going to attack you, so you jacked the bird-shot shells out of your shotgun, fumbled in your pockets, found rifled slug rounds you just happened to have, loaded them into your gun and shot the bear before he could attack you? Is that it?"

"That's it," said Billy.

Brennan's inclination was to pursue the matter further, but then he thought better of it. Billy had simply spotted a bear and shot it, and Brennan knew that any judge would see it that way. So, he wrapped things up, explaining to the Treadwells that they would receive in the mail notices to appear in court.

Brennan left that evening content in the knowledge that he would never have to return there again. But he was to revisit the case now and then in his memory, and it would always result in a chuckle. The Treadwells, he concluded, had been the most unskilled liars he had ever encountered. One absurd story had followed another.

But the best story of all had come on that afternoon Brennan paid his third visit to their home, when they at first wouldn't open the door. Apparently thinking that Brennan might simply go away, they didn't answer until Brennan had nearly pounded the door off its hinges. Thinking Brennan would be mad about it, they had hastily concocted what they considered to be the perfect story to explain their delay in answering the door. Brenda delivered the story with a coy smile.

"We couldn't get the door right away because we were in the shower."

Brennan stared at them in disbelief, then he nearly strangled suppressing laughter as he regarded his two suspects who, according to their story, had just stepped from the shower. It would have been a better alibi, Brennan thought, had they not been standing before him fully dressed, with dry hair.

Trouble in Hog Heaven

The transaction took place in the dead of night, on a lonely dirt road off Interstate 5. The lights of Bakersfield gleamed faintly in the distance. A bobtail truck emblazoned with the words *Goins Creek Hunting Club, Inc.* in bright red letters was parked at an abandoned cattle yard, its sliding side cargo door open against the mouth of a wooden loading chute. A few yards away, a big diesel pickup had backed a horse trailer to a small corral adjoining the chute. Two lean men in western garb stood beside the trailer, their sweat-stained hats pulled low over their eyes.

But neither horses nor cattle charged from the trailer when the cowboys flung open its rear doors. First to burst out was a large and furious wild boar, over 200 pounds of bad news. It was a European strain, heavy through the shoulders with relatively small hindquarters. It bolted first one way, then another in the small corral, jaws popping with rage, moonlight glinting off its murderous white tusks.

"He's a good one," said one of the cowboys. "We want two hundred for him."

Randy Goins, of the Goins Creek Hunting Club, readily agreed to the price and studied the other pigs that followed the large boar from the trailer—a smaller boar and three sows. Following a brief discussion, Goins paid for the pigs, peeling bills from a large wad of cash. Like a drug deal in the night, the transaction was a criminal act, for it was illegal in California to buy or sell wild pigs or even to possess them alive.

Randy questioned them briefly about how they had captured the pigs and how they got them into a horse trailer.

"We bay 'em with dogs, then rope 'em," answered one of the cowboys, but he declined to say more, obviously displeased over being questioned at all. He and his companion used long-handled electric prods to haze the pigs up the wooden chute and into the bobtail truck. With that, Randy slid the door shut on the bobtail. He and the cowboys parted company in opposite directions.

As Randy headed back for the interstate, the pigs rode in silence, huddled together in one corner of the bobtail's large cargo bay, their tiny pig-eyes probing the utter darkness.

***

It was a collection of little things that ultimately drew the attention of the game wardens to the Goins Creek Hunting Club. There was secondhand information from a Los Angeles County Sheriff's Department deputy, whose brother-in-law had hunted there and mentioned seeing what looked like baited areas and wild pigs in pens.

There were also observations by the warden who worked the northern slopes of the Tehachapi Mountains. He had become suspicious when the locks were changed on the gates to the Goins Ranch and the Goins men, a father and his two sons, no longer welcomed wardens on their vast acreage. The warden's requests for keys for the new locks were always stalled or put off. Then there were rumors of guided hunts on the ranch, and a check with Fish and Game license staff revealed that none of the Goins clan had guide's licenses. The sum total of all of these things resulted in the notification of Fish and Game's Special Operations Unit, or SOU, as it is known.

One November morning at SOU's headquarters office in Sacramento, Lt. Eddy Watkins presided over a small group of warden undercover operatives in a round-table discussion of potential SOU projects. Open in front of him was a file folder marked *Goins Creek Hunting Club*.

Watkins was a retired narcotics officer from the Los Angeles Police Department. For 20 years he not only endured the absolute worst the battleground streets of LA could dish out, he thrived on it. Upon his retirement from LAPD, he had become a game warden. The Department of Fish and Game, quick to recognize the value of his vast experience in covert operations, promptly put him in charge of the newly-formed SOU. Those with whom he worked soon learned to regard him with absolute respect.

"What do you think?" said Watkins. "Do these people deserve a closer look?"

Among those present was Roy Griffith, a superb young warden who was five years into his career and loving it. During his two years with SOU, Griffith had distinguished himself. Experiencing some of the finest adventures of his life, he had worked undercover successfully against some of the most dangerous and destructive outlaws in the western states. Griffith thought highly of Watkins, who he described as a cross between his favorite uncle and John Wayne.

"I get a bad feeling about these people," said Griffith. "I think we should book a bird hunt with them." The other wardens agreed, and Watkins considered the decision.

"Okay, Roy," he finally said. "Go ahead and set it up. Maybe I'll go with you."

Later that day, Griffith phoned the Goins Ranch, and introduced himself, using his undercover name, Roy Gross.

"I represent Keystone Investments Company in LA," said Griffith. "I'm interested in hunting opportunities."

The man on the line introduced himself as Lester Goins. "My sons and I own the ranch and the hunting club. What type of hunting do you like?"

Griffith then delivered his cover story, that his company, Keystone Investments, often entertained wealthy investors, and he was looking for a place he could bring them to hunt.

"We want a place where there's lots of game and our clients won't have to work too hard to get it. If your club turns out to be what we're looking for, we'll consider a corporate membership."

Griffith concluded the conversation by booking a one-day chukar hunt for early December. Operation Pig Caper had begun.

Watkins decided to accompany Griffith on the chukar hunt, and on the chosen morning, shortly before 8 a.m., they arrived at the Goins Ranch. They were met there by the ranch caretaker, who introduced himself as Bud Shanks.

"There's been a mixup," said Shanks. "Mr. Goins had to be away on business, so I'll be showing you where to hunt."

Before they left the clubhouse, they met Randy Goins, one of Lester's sons. They asked him questions about the club and inquired about the possibility of pig hunting.

"This ranch is hog heaven," said Randy. "And they're the best of the wild strain. We don't plant any domestic pigs here."

The wardens hunted that morning, and when they had shot enough birds to support their cover story, they set out on a foot reconnaissance. They covered as much ground as they could through the sage and scattered oaks, and it turned out to be worth the hike. First, they encountered a scattered pile of corncobs and produce remnants.

"This is a bait pile," said Griffith. "It's been fed down pretty much, but it's still a bait pile."

Farther on by a water hole, they discovered a large box trap. It contained corncobs and large animal bones and was large enough to trap either bear or pigs, but it was not set.

Their most interesting find, however, was a huge orange pile of over 1,000 pounds of carrots, obviously meant to bait pigs.

On their way back to the clubhouse, they came upon the carcasses of a number of dead cows. Their suspicion that it was another pig-bait station was substantiated that afternoon when Shanks took them for a Jeep tour of the ranch. When Griffith asked about the cows, Shanks replied, "We have a neighbor dump his dead cows there. They're for the pigs to chew on. They'll eat anything."

The wardens were surprised by his answer, and were further surprised when Shanks drove them by another huge pile of carrots, and a mechanical grain dispenser as well. Such baiting machines were legal to hunt over in some eastern states, but not California, where baiting of any kind was against the law. But Shanks hadn't hesitated to mention that both the carrots and the grain were for the hogs.

Upon leaving the ranch that afternoon, the wardens discussed what they had seen that day.

"What amazes me most," said Griffith, "is that they're so open about what they're doing. It's like they're totally unconcerned about the law." Then he added, "I think it's time they were educated."

The following morning, Griffith received a pager call from a woman who booked hunts for the Goins Ranch.

"Mr. Goins is sorry that he couldn't be there yesterday," she said. "He really wanted to meet you. And I wanted to tell you about a special we're having in January. Two-day meat-hog hunts are going to be $300 instead of $400. Griffith told her that he would probably be contacting her after the first of the year to arrange for a pig hunt.

As it happened, it wasn't until February that Griffith next visited the Goins Ranch. He came a day early and checked into the Travelodge Motel in Tehachapi, where he and Watkins had stayed before. When he was settled into his room, he brought out his month's-end paperwork, hoping to catch up. He laid out a variety of Fish and Game forms and reports, spreading them across his bed. No sooner was he immersed in the paperwork when there came a knock at his door. Upon approaching the door and peering through the peephole, he was horrified to see Randy Goins standing there.

"Just a minute," he cried as he turned and frantically snatched up his paperwork, stuffing it under the bedcovers. Then he spotted his undercover handgun and stashed it under a pillow. He took five seconds to compose himself before he opened the door, looking sleepy-eyed, as though just awakened from a nap.

"Oh, Randy, it's you!" he said, offering his right hand. "Come in."

"Thought I'd stop by and check on you," said Randy, returning the handshake. "Do you have time for a drink? We could go over a few things about our hunt tomorrow."

Griffith agreed, and sat to put on his shoes. Randy plopped down in a chair and peered around the room. Griffith held his breath, hoping he hadn't missed something that would give him away. But Randy seemed unconcerned by anything he saw.

It was a tense situation, and Griffith learned a valuable lesson. From then on, Griffith would purge his vehicle and baggage of anything that could give him away during an undercover operation. This precaution paid off a year later when he gave a rather dangerous suspect a ride in his pickup. During the ride, the wary suspect said he needed a pen and popped open Griffith's glove compartment. Griffith saw him find a pen, but continue to search. Fortunately, Griffith had left him nothing to find.

"We'll need to start early," said Randy, later over drinks. "At first light we'll be sitting on a rock overlooking the carrot pile. We'll try to get a hog before they make it back into the dense brush. The hogs have been really hammering the carrots. We've been going through ten tons every two weeks."

Again, Griffith was amazed that Randy would talk so freely about the illegal practice of baiting and hunting near a bait pile.

The following morning, Griffith was there at 4:45 a.m. He and Randy hopped into a Jeep and headed out, and on the way to the carrot pile Randy gave Griffith further instructions.

"Keep your gun loaded with one in the chamber. If you see any coyotes or mountain lions, shoot them. They really raise hell with the deer herd." The fact that lions were fully protected under California law obviously didn't concern him.

Suddenly several pigs dashed across the road in the headlights.

"Jump out and get ready," said Randy, and when Griffith was out of the vehicle, Randy directed the Jeep's headlights in sweeping arcs up the hillside where the pigs had run. In so doing, he violated yet another state law. Griffith also noted that it was a full 45 minutes prior to legal shooting time. But the hogs escaped, and the two men continued on their way.

They found no pigs at the carrot pile, and Randy decided it was time to leave the Jeep and hunt on foot.

"Here," said Randy, plucking a branch from a low shrub. "Rub some sage on your clothes. It will help mask your scent from the hogs." Griffith did as instructed. Soon, they spotted pigs on a hillside about 400 yards away. Their attempt to stalk them failed. They walked and walked, until they finally broke for lunch.

Shortly before dark, they headed out in the Jeep to drive back and check the main carrot pile.

"I've been watching you," said Randy, glancing at Griffith as they drove. "I've been sizing you up . . . and I'm convinced you're not some kind of animal rights wacko. So we can do whatever you want. I mean we can guarantee you a pig, anytime you want one. We've got pigs we kind of get on the black market. Some crazy cowboys up by King City catch them for us. Then they call us, and we haggle over the price. Then we meet 'em halfway and pick up the pigs."

As they approached the carrot pile, several pigs appeared in the headlights.

"Get ready!" said Randy, but the pigs darted into the brush and were gone. Randy again swept the Jeep's headlights over area into which the pigs disappeared, but they saw nothing. Griffith made a mental note of yet another violation of the state's anti-spotlighting law.

"Pigs aren't like deer," said Randy. "They don't freeze when you shine a spotlight on 'em."

Back at the clubhouse, Lester Goins, a hard-looking, intimidating man in his late 50s, was there with his oldest son, Kevin. Griffith discussed with them his hunt that day and asked about the carrots.

"They eat 'em up as fast as I put 'em out. We've got a guy that brings 'em in for us, a standing deal. The carrots keep the sows down low, and that brings the boars down." Griffith added this information to his growing mental store of evidence against the Goins clan.

Later that night, Griffith met Randy for dinner in town, and they discussed the hunt for the following day.

"Tomorrow, anything goes . . . spotlighting, whatever. We're going to get you a pig."

But most of the following day proved to be much like the ones before—a failure, from Randy's standpoint, but productive for Griffith in his evidence gathering. This was particularly true when they passed stout pens not far from the clubhouse.

"You should see the wild pigs we have in *there*," said Randy.

"I'd like to see 'em," said Griffith.

"Maybe later," said Randy. "I really shouldn't show you."

Later in the day, they passed the pens again.

"When do I get to see what those wild pigs look like?" said Griffith. Randy studied Griffith for a few seconds, then stopped the Jeep near the pens and motioned for Griffith to get out and follow him. Inside one of the pens were five adult pigs, all black, and a litter of five young ones. All but one large boar appeared to be terrified of the men.

"These are some of the ones we get from the cowboys in King City," said Randy. "One of the sows was pregnant."

Just then, the big boar charged the fence, striking it with a crash. Both men jumped back.

"That's the meanest, wildest pig I've ever seen," said Randy, and as they walked back to the Jeep he said, "You didn't see those, okay?"

"I didn't see a thing," said Griffith.

Late that afternoon, following a meal at the clubhouse, they took the Jeep and again headed for the big carrot pile. They left the Jeep at dusk and took up a position in the sage, about 40 yards from the carrot pile. Randy carried a Marlin .444 caliber lever-action rifle.

"If we see pigs, it'll be kind of a team thing. I'll say one, two, three, and we'll shoot. I'll back you up to make sure we get a good kill."

When it was nearly too dark to see, Griffith spotted three pigs walking up the road to the carrot pile. He pointed them out to Randy, who told him to pick the one he wanted.

"I'm gonna take number three," whispered Griffith.

"Okay, one . . . two . . . *three*," said Randy, and both rifles boomed. Griffith's pig ran about 10 yards and collapsed. Randy took off after the survivors. When they approached the downed pig, both men were surprised at the size of it.

"That's a trophy pig, the purest strain of wild pig I've ever seen come off of the ranch," said Randy. "Boy, my dad's gonna be upset. You paid for a meat-pig and you shot a trophy boar."

Randy was correct that his father would be upset, and his older brother Kevin was angry as well. After the pig had been hauled back to the clubhouse, Lester Goins threw a minor tantrum aimed at Randy.

"Why did you let him shoot a big boar?" he said. "That's a $1,500 trophy boar!"

Then, turning to Griffith, he said, "You weren't supposed to shoot a trophy boar."

"There were only three pigs," said Griffith. "Randy told me to pick one and shoot it. It was too dark to really see 'em."

"Well, we'll have to charge more money for that pig."

"Hey, I paid for a meat-pig, and that's what I want," said Griffith. "You can *keep* this one."

There was much grumbling and complaining by the older of the two Goins, but in the end, they thought it best to let Griffith keep the pig.

The following day, Watkins listened with interest as Griffith detailed his latest experiences, enumerating the various violations he had substantiated.

"We could take Randy right now for hunting over bait, night hunting, spotlighting, guiding without a license, and his illegal possession of the live pigs," said Griffith. "But I'd like to make sure that *Daddy* Goins goes down as well. He's the *real* culprit. And we shouldn't forget the other brother." Watkins was in complete agreement.

Two weeks later, Griffith returned to the Goins Ranch. Watkins was again with him, and another man as well. Henry Kim was a native of the US, but both of his parents had immigrated from Korea. On this day, Kim was on loan to SOU from the Los Angeles Police Department's Asian Crimes Task

Force. He was one of Watkins' many contacts from LAPD, and he was a superb undercover operative.

Upon their arrival, Watkins introduced Kim to the Goins men, using Kim's undercover name.

"This is Steven Lee," said Watkins. "He's here to hunt."

"I want to shoot big pig for my father!" said Kim with a broad grin. "This year of Golden Boar!" Kim delivered these words with a right-off-the-boat Korean accent, which entertained the wardens, for Kim normally spoke perfect, accent-free English.

"Well, you've come to the right place," said Lester.

Kim and the wardens had arrived late one afternoon, expecting Kim to shoot his pig the following day as part of what Lester described to Watkins as "a canned hunt." But because there was still daylight left, Lester suggested that they visit the carrot pile in hopes that Kim could get a shot at a pig.

Pigs did arrive at the carrot pile just before dark. This was bad luck for the wardens, for they wanted to catch Lester and his sons conducting their canned and highly illegal hunt planned for the next day. If Kim shot a pig on this evening, the canned hunt would be off. This, however, was not a problem for Kim, a crack shot, who upon being directed by Lester to shoot, intentionally sent his 180-grain bullet into the dirt, beneath the pig's belly. The pigs scattered, and Lester was not happy.

"I very nervous," Kim explained.

The following morning, Lester Goins again took Kim to the carrot pile in hopes of getting Kim a pig without resorting to the more expensive option of the canned hunt. The pigs failed to cooperate, but the Jeep ride there and back was highly rewarding for the wardens. Lester drove, with Kim to his right, and Griffith and Watkins rode in the back seat. Griffith carried a camcorder to film the hunt, but when Lester became very talkative during the ride to the carrot pile, Griffith began secretly filming from the back seat. In doing so, he recorded Lester in some highly incriminating conversation with Watkins, words that Lester would regret for years. Lester in effect summarized his and his sons' illegal pursuits—the baiting, the buying and selling of trapped pigs, the night hunting, all of it—in such a way that no one could doubt that they knew perfectly well that they were committing numerous criminal acts. At one point, he even commented on game wardens.

"You gotta watch out for those damned Fish and Game boys. They try to infiltrate you . . . you know, entrapment. We have to be real careful."

Back at the clubhouse, Watkins met with Lester alone to discussed plans for the canned, guaranteed pig killing that would occur that afternoon. What Watkins heard sickened him.

"It's all set up, but we had some problems," said Lester. "We cut tendons in the hind legs of a boar so he couldn't run . . . so he would stay at the carrot pile. But he could still move too well, so we had to tie him to a tree. When your man shoots the pig, you have to keep him back for a minute or two so we have time to untie him and hide the rope." Watkins agreed to the plan, successfully masking his disgust. He then paid for the hunt, handing Lester six $100 bills.

The canned hunt went down exactly as Lester and sons had planned it. Lester led Kim to a spot overlooking the carrot pile while Griffith and Watkins trailed a few yards behind. Griffith was filming the entire event. Kevin was waiting for them there and whispered that a good size boar was asleep under a tree near the carrot pile. He then led Kim a few yards closer, pointed out the boar to him and directed him to steady his rifle against a tree for the shot. Kim did as directed, took careful aim through the scope and squeezed the trigger. The rifle bucked with the shot, and the sad ordeal of the hamstrung boar was ended.

Kevin and Lester immediately sprinted toward the boar, having ordered Kim to stay put for a minute. Griffith continued filming, zooming in, as Kevin knelt beside the hog, hurriedly untied it, and covered the rope with brush at the base of the tree.

"Can you believe that?" said Watkins quietly as he, Kim and Griffith walked forward. "We got 'em by the short hairs now!"

Lester and his sons made a big deal out of the kill, praising Kim's fine shooting skills and repeatedly photographing Kim, rifle in hand, grinning from ear to ear, posing with the dead boar. Griffith continued filming, including footage of Lester, Kevin and even Watkins posing with Kim over the boar. Following the photograph session, Randy and Kevin skinned and quartered the boar and packed the meat in meat sacks.

When Kim and the wardens departed that evening, Lester and his sons saw them off. "Will we be seeing you again soon?" Lester inquired. Griffith cheerfully provided the answer.

"You can count on it!" he said with a smile.

The Goins men would indeed see the wardens again soon. Two days later, six Fish and Game patrol vehicles convoyed onto the ranch, and over a dozen wardens jumped out and scattered to surround the ranch headquarters and clubhouse. Hearing the commotion, Randy walked out to stare at the wardens with confusion. Then Griffith approached him, search warrant in hand.

"Bad news, Randy," said Griffith. Then it dawned on the man, and he appeared to wilt.

The wardens documented everything, photographing bait stations, traps and wild pigs in pens. They seized records into evidence from the clubs files documenting numerous illegally guided and fraudulently conducted hunts, plus notes and records of cash payments for the purchase of illegally captured wild pigs.

The resulting case was a slam-dunk, magnificently prepared and presented by Griffith. Of the many charges against the Goins, one particularly struck fear into their hearts, for the brutal act of hamstringing Kim's wild boar was a clear case of cruelty to animals, which was a serious, no-guns-for-you-anymore felony. They quickly hired a prominent defense attorney who represented them at their preliminary hearing.

On that day, the Goins men and their attorney waited in a hallway adjoining the courtroom for their case to be called. Griffith was also present, and he witnessed something that greatly amused him. Lester Goins began to berate his son Randy for talking too much to the clients who had turned out to be undercover wardens. But their attorney, a pony-tailed weasel in Gucci shoes and a $2,000 suit, approached Lester, put a firm hand on his shoulder and said, "Mr. Goins, you've apparently not seen the warden's videotape." This was in reference to Griffith's secret film shot during the Jeep ride. In it, a highly talkative Lester himself provided more than enough incriminating information to hang the entire family.

Later, the attorney approached Griffith with a sincere compliment. "Warden Griffith, if the narcotics officers who arrest most of my clients did as thorough and professional a job as you have done in preparing this case, I'd be out of business. We want to settle this. Mr. Goins and his sons will do anything to avoid facing trial on the felony charge. What do you want?"

What Griffith wanted, and what he got, was more than enough to ensure the Goins people would never again risk abusing the game laws. They would make monthly payments to Fish and Game on their staggering fines for years, and they would be placed on searchable probation with orders to provide the wardens with keys to all locks and total access to their property.

Griffith was left with good memories of the case, but Watkins and Henry Kim were to have something more tangible. Two months after the arrests, Kim received a large package in the mail. Upon opening it, he had a great laugh. His gift from Griffith was the meticulously cleaned and dried skull of the boar he had shot. Griffith had spray-painted the hideous-looking thing gold and inscribed upon it *The Year of the Golden Boar*.

Watkins too received a gift from Griffith, a large framed photo. Griffith, during one day of his undercover hunt, had somehow convinced Randy Goins to snap the photo. Watkins laughed when he saw it, for it was of a widely grinning Griffith, rifle in hand, perched atop a giant pile of carrots. An inscription beneath the photo read, *Bait pile? What bait pile?*

The Cycle

She lived underwater where the ocean met the shore, in the violent intertidal world of rugged rocks and surging current. One of the sea's least dynamic creatures, she hardly moved, but clung to a granite face in a deep crevice between two boulders, feeding on bits of drifting kelp and other algae.

Biologists classified her as a marine snail, but most would recognize her as an abalone. To those who had experienced the delicate flavor of her kind, of the muscular "foot" with which they attach themselves to rocks, abalone were considered among the most delicious creatures on earth, a fact which placed her in constant danger.

She was huge for her species, her flat, shallow shell more than 10 inches across. She had grown large because she had always remained deep in her crevice, beyond the reach of sea otters or the prowling abalone divers who longed to slip a steel bar beneath her to pry her from the rock face.

But conditions had changed, and the food she depended upon had become scarce. So now, at her snail's pace, she abandoned her safe place and moved toward the crevice opening where food was more abundant. In so doing, she placed herself in grave peril.

***

It was not yet dawn as a small, foreign-made sedan pulled off the coast highway into the empty parking lot at Franklin Point. Doors flew open and two compact young men stepped out. The driver remained behind the wheel. Hurrying to the rear of the vehicle, the two men popped the trunk and grabbed heavy bags of gear. They slammed the trunk, shot hurried words to the driver in some Asian tongue, shouldered the bags and headed down the narrow trail to the ocean. The driver immediately pulled out of the parking lot and headed down the highway.

Upon reaching their chosen destination at the water's edge, the two men pulled on wetsuits and weight belts, grabbed other loose gear including abalone irons, mesh game bags and waterproof flashlights. They then made their way through the slippery rocks and eelgrass, into the water. The ocean was flat-calm, the tide unusually low.

The abalone were there in numbers, as the men knew they would be. Selecting the larger ones, red abalone of seven inches or larger, they began the harvest. With deft strokes of the abalone irons, flat steel bars often called "ab irons," they popped abalone after abalone off of the rocks and placed them in the mesh game bags.

It was no surprise that abalone were so plentiful there, for that part of the California coast, south of San Francisco, had been closed to the taking of abalone for years. The two men were aware of this fact, but they were aware also that each illegal abalone they took could be readily sold in San Francisco for over $75.

As they continued working, one of the men directed his light into a deep crevice between two boulders and grunted in surprise as he spotted the largest abalone he had ever seen. It had to be over 10 inches wide. But it was deep in the crevice, only barely within reach of his abalone iron. He knew he would have just one chance at it, for upon a missed attempt with his ab iron, he knew the animal would suck itself tight onto the rock and be impossible to dislodge from its difficult location.

The man prepared himself, planned his move, then thrust with his ab iron. The flattened point of the iron slipped easily between the abalone and the rock face, and the man had just enough room for a quick pry with the bar. The abalone, taken by surprise, lost her grip and fell free. The man, now straining to reach as far into the crevice as he could, was barely able to reach the fallen abalone with the very tip of his iron. Carefully, he raked the abalone toward him until he was just able to grab it. He then pulled it out, examined it in the first gray light of dawn and again grunted with amazement over its magnificent size.

***

Dawn was just breaking as Lt. Don Kelly, Department of Fish and Game, pulled his green patrol rig off Highway 101, into the parking lot at Franklin Point. He swung through the lot, and upon seeing neither people nor vehicles, he pulled back onto the highway and headed north.

But Kelly wasn't gone long. After a half hour of checking other spots up the coast for the abalone poachers he knew the minus tide would attract, he headed back to Franklin Point. This time he found a small, foreign-made sedan parked there. Stepping from his patrol rig, he approached the sedan and touched its hood. Still warm. He peered down the trail leading down to the beach, but no one was in sight.

Kelly returned to his patrol rig and drove a short distance down the highway, then turned off at a point where he could conceal his vehicle. Then he grabbed some gear and set out on foot. He soon reached a clifftop from which he had clear view of Franklin Point and the rocky beach area below and around it, the area in which poachers would most likely be in action.

In a hidden spot amid dense vegetation, Kelly set up a spotting scope on a stout tripod and began glassing the area. Despite a light, early morning fog, he immediately spotted a lone man standing atop the cliffs over the rocky beach. Studying the man, Kelly noticed that he was nervously looking around, peering back at the parking lot and apparently studying the trails and surrounding clifftops. He would then look down at the beach and sometimes wave his hat in that direction.

Obviously a lookout, Kelly thought.

At about this time, Kelly's portable radio came alive on his belt, and he heard wardens Chad Alexander and Jess Mitchell announce that they were in service. Kelly immediately radioed the two wardens, explained that he almost certainly had a violation in progress. Alexander and Mitchell were not far away, and they immediately headed in Kelly's direction.

Kelly now returned his attention to the lookout. The man was smoking cigarettes, one after the other, pacing back and forth, and looking in all directions, obviously keeping watch. Kelly was certain one or more suspects were in the water somewhere along the rocky shoreline, up to no good, poaching abalone, but he couldn't find them. High rocks prevented his seeing much of the most likely areas that the poachers would be working. He searched and searched with his spotting scope, but to no avail.

Then he found that the lookout had disappeared. The man had left his post, and Kelly had no idea which way he had gone. Kelly radioed Alexander and Mitchell and advised them of the situation. They had arrived at the parking lot, parked out of sight and had the foreign-made sedan under surveillance.

Ten minutes later, Kelly spotted movement on one of the trails leading up from the beach. Training his spotting scope on the area, he saw three men bearing heavy packs, trudging up the trail. Looking closer, Kelly recognized one of them as the missing lookout. Kelly advised the other wardens, providing them the lookout's clothing description, and watched as the suspects hiked up the steep trail. Then they were around a bend in the trail and out of his sight.

It was another 10 minutes before the suspects reappeared, cautiously approaching the parking lot. When they reached their car, Alexander suddenly stepped into view in full uniform, giving them a good fright.

"State game wardens," announced Alexander. "What have you men been doing?" At that moment, the suspects noticed that a second uniformed warden had stepped out of cover behind them and was approaching.

The wardens towered over the three suspects, men of small stature who stood wide-eyed, gulping air. Finally one of them found his voice.

"We are on vacation," he said in accented English.

The lookout, who Alexander was able to identify from Kelly's description, was wearing a large backpack.

"What's in the pack?" asked Alexander.

The lookout slipped the pack from his back and set it on the ground.

"Can I look inside?" asked Alexander. It was worded as a question, but none present saw it that way.

The lookout nodded for Alexander to look inside the pack. Alexander did so, and inside he found two wetsuits, two pairs of diving booties, and other diving gear.

"What were you doing with the wetsuits?" Alexander inquired.

"We were just swimming in them," said one of the suspects. "We're on vacation."

"Do you have any other gear with you? Anything you might have left back down the trail?" Alexander pressed.

The suspects now looked at one another then acted as though they didn't understand the question. But both wardens had played this game before, the "me no speak the language" routine, and both had no doubts that the suspects understood every word.

Ignoring the lookout, Alexander now turned to the other two suspects.

"Did you two men wear the wetsuits?"

They nodded their heads and one of them answered, "Yes." Alexander noted that the hands of both men were red and marred with scratches, sure proof that they were indeed the divers.

Lt. Kelly now arrived on the scene, and Alexander and Mitchell advised him of what they had learned from the suspects.

"Your lookout was carrying the wetsuits, but the others were the divers," said Mitchell. "They're all being evasive with us."

Kelly now turned to the suspects and asked them if they had left any gear or anything else back along the trail. But the suspects feigned ignorance and did not answer.

"One last chance," said Kelly. "If you left abalone or anything else along the trail, you need to tell us now." But the suspects continued to play dumb.

Kelly now directed Alexander to remain with the suspects, and he and Mitchell set off down the trail to look for hidden evidence. Their initial search revealed nothing, so they turned back for a more careful search.

Then Kelly made an important observation: The damp morning had left tiny droplets of dew on the leaves and stems of all the trailside vegetation. This was important, because suddenly he stopped, noticing a place along the trail where the dew on some vegetation had been disturbed. He carefully followed the trail of disturbed dew on vegetation for about 30 feet before he came to a place where long grass had been pulled down to conceal something. Pushing it aside, Kelly revealed two heavy backpacks jammed with large abalone.

In the meantime, Alexander had separated the lookout from other two suspects and was working on him, attempting to turn him against the others. The lookout stood looking at his feet as the warden spoke to him.

"You know," said Alexander, "You don't have to go down with these guys. They're going to jail for a long time. You were just the lookout. You could cooperate with us and help yourself."

The color had drained from the lookout's face and he now began to dry heave, on the verge of vomiting. But Alexander knew that the man would never cooperate with the wardens.

Kelly and Mitchell now arrived bearing the two heavy packs of abalone. They dumped the packs onto the ground at the feet of the suspects, and out tumbled what turned out to be 56 large abalone. There were also two abalone irons, a crowbar and two flashlights, one of which was turned on and shining brightly. Kelly then approached the two divers and said, "You men are under arrest."

Alexander and Mitchell restrained the two divers, pulling their arms behind their backs and applying the handcuffs. Soon thereafter, they were seat-belted in patrol vehicles and on their way to the county jail in Redwood City, a good hour away. The lookout was luckier. For his less serious part in the crime, he was issued a citation and allowed to leave.

Kelly then began sorting through the abalone, placing them in two piles. Those that were uninjured, with no cuts or broken shells, were to be released. The others would not survive and would be retained as evidence.

When Alexander and Mitchell arrived in Redwood City, they faced a problem. Many of the streets of the town were blocked off due to a Fourth of July parade in progress, and there was no way to get to the jail. The wardens considered the problem for a bit then discovered that there actually *was* a way to get to the jail. They could join the parade.

And so it was that parade viewers on that day got an extra treat as two fully marked Fish and Game patrol vehicles cruised sedately by, their uniformed drivers smiling and waving to the crowd. Their handcuffed passengers, however, were not nearly so cheerful.

***

Months later, after the suspects pled not guilty, the case went to jury trial. It was a case that could easily have been lost, for Kelly had not actually seen the two divers taking abalone. But a very determined and talented prosecuting attorney, a young woman by the name of Shin-Mee Chang, saw to it that the violators paid the price for their crimes. Superbly prepared, Prosecutor Chang systematically destroyed the case for the defense.

It was an unusual trial, with each suspect wearing a headset and in almost constant, audible communication in Cantonese with an interpreter. Following three days of trial, all three suspects were found guilty.

So grateful were the wardens over Shin-Mee Chang's magnificent courtroom performance on an important case that Kelly later presented her with a framed letter of commendation.

A few weeks after the convictions, an unsympathetic judge sentenced the poachers to permanent loss of their commercial and sport fishing rights, a month in jail and heavy fines. The convicted men blinked in sad realization as it dawned on them that they could never again fish or pick abalone in California.

Justice had been served.

***

A mere three hours after the poachers had waded ashore at Franklin Point with the 56 poached abalone, 35 of the illegally harvested abalone were returned to their watery home. Lt. Don Kelly personally took care of the task, aided by a local ranger.

With great care, the two men placed each abalone in a good spot, holding them against rock surfaces in protected places until they could reattach.

Kelly took particular care with a very large one, a female whose flat shell measured over 10 inches across. He found a deep crevice, pushed her as far back as he could reach, then held her there until he felt her take hold of the crevice wall.

Before the year would end, the big female abalone would emit over 15 million eggs through the pores in her beautiful shell, eggs that would float free in the water to unite with the millions of sperm broadcast there by males of her species.

Of the millions of resulting fertilized eggs, only a few would survive to adulthood, but this would be enough to begin the cycle anew. At least for now, the species would continue.

The Caviar Connection

A moonless winter night.

Vang Xiong could smell the river and its muddy edges, a dank, earthy smell that he found strangely pleasant. It reminded him of the Mekong River of his youth, a wide stream he had last swum for the last time with bullets striking the surface around him. But there were no bullets here. No war. Just the quiet whisper of moving water between wooded banks.

By the light of his campfire, Xiong tested the drag on his heavy fishing reel, its line snaking up through the guides on his rod, then down into the dark water of the river. The reel's clicker buzzed like an angry rattler as he pulled out a foot of line. Then he placed the rod in a rod holder jammed into the ground, tightened the line and again settled down to wait.

The big fish were there, deep beneath the river's surface, but never in great numbers. Survivors from the age of dinosaurs, they resembled sharks. But instead of flesh-ripping, tooth-studded jaws, theirs were harmless ventral mouths, like vacuum cleaners, which scoured the river bottom for protein of any kind. Anything but pretty, the white sturgeon were indeed relics of the past, among the most enduring creatures to ever inhabit the earth.

An older female of the species, not far below Xiong's camp, caught the scent of something edible and headed for it. The source of the scent was several grass shrimp impaled on a large hook. The fish located the bait with ease and immediately inhaled it, hook and all. She then moved away at a leisurely pace.

Xiong leaped up as the rod bent and the reel began to buzz. Snatching up the rod, he counted to 10 before flipping the reel into gear and throwing his whole body into a violent jerk with the rod, setting the hook.

Upon feeling the bite of steel, the big fish shot away like a fired torpedo. Xiong's reel shrieked, and his rod bent in a tight arc. The fish ended her initial run with a magnificent leap, clearing the water by four feet. She landed with a great splash and shot away again.

But experience and technology were on Xiong's side, for he had fought many big fish, and his heavy fishing gear easily handled the fish's powerful runs. It was 15 minutes before the fish began to noticeably tire, and another 20 before Xiong battled it into the shallows where his cousin could snag it with a long-handled gaff. Together, Xiong and his cousin dragged the great fish onto the bank where it lay exhausted, gills pulsing, considerably longer than Xiong was tall. With its long, ugly snout and armored body, it looked more reptile than fish.

Following a phone call the next morning, Xiong drove to a Sacramento parking lot where he met with a middle-aged woman, who spoke broken English with a heavy Russian accent. The butchered sturgeon was in the back of Xiong's pickup, as were plastic bags containing about three gallons of sturgeon roe. There was no haggling, just a quick transaction. The woman counted cash into Xiong's hand, and Xiong helped her load the fish and roe into the trunk of her car. They then went their separate ways.

***

He was known as Cajun Bob, a sturgeon fisherman, one of the regulars at the hot fishing spots on the Sacramento River. The game wardens, however, referred to him as the Ragin' Cajun, due to his tirades when he would call to report the wrongdoings of others. The wardens always suspected that he was as crooked as those on whom he informed. But he occasionally came across with good information, so the wardens tolerated him.

Such was the case one late winter's day when he contacted Warden Troy Bruce of California's Wildlife Protection Special Investigations Unit, or SOU. Bruce listened with growing interest as the outraged Ragin' Cajun made his report.

"They're buying sturgeon," said Cajun Bob. "They tried to buy one from me, and when I said no, they asked if they could buy the eggs. They were talkin' to everyone on the river. It was a woman and a younger man, some kind of foreigners."

Bruce extracted all of the useful information he could from the man, then asked him to call immediately if the sturgeon buyers showed up again. This was not the first Bruce had heard of the illegal selling of California sturgeon. He was not surprised. In fact, he had expected it, in view of to the condition of the Russian caviar industry in recent years. In Russia, the sturgeon population along the Caspian Sea had been dangerously overharvested, creating a worldwide shortage of beluga caviar.

Bruce was interested enough in Cajun Bob's report that he discussed it with Lt. Nancy Foley, the head of SOU at the time. Both agreed that the matter deserved a hard look. Soon thereafter, undercover wardens with sturgeon gear were sent to various places along the Sacramento River to fish for sturgeon and hopefully to be approached by the illegal buyers.

But nothing happened. Weeks passed, and none of the undercover wardens were contacted by anyone interested in buying fish or roe. After a full month, Foley decided to call off the operation.

But soon thereafter, Cajun Bob was approached again, and he had done as Bruce had instructed him and asked for a contact telephone number.

"I'll give you a call if I get a nice fish," he had told them.

Cajun Bob then contacted Bruce and provided the warden with a slip of paper bearing the name Vladimir and a Sacramento phone number.

Bruce now met again with Foley, and they decided that they had nothing to lose by calling Vladimir and trying to gain his confidence and arrange for a covert sale. It was early February of 2002 when Bruce made the call. A woman answered in heavily accented English and passed the phone to the man Bruce would come to know as Vladimir.

"I'm a sturgeon fisherman," said Bruce. "I heard you pay money for sturgeon. I don't have a fish right now, but I can get one."

The man was wary at first, but Bruce said all the right things and skillfully gained his trust.

"I pay $15 a pound for roe and $1.50 to $2 for meat," said Vladimir.

"That's good," said Bruce. "I'll call you when I get a fish. Remember, my name is Troy."

Two days later, wardens in the Delta seized a 74-inch sturgeon from an angler who had ignored the 72-inch maximum size limit that protects the important brood stock females. The big fish was sent to SOU for use in their covert operation.

Upon obtaining the fish, Bruce phoned Vladimir, who wanted to know if the fish was male or female.

"I don't know," said Bruce. "But I have it in the back of my pickup. Do you want it?"

Vladimir agreed to meet Bruce to look at the fish. Bruce, wearing a transmitting listening device, or wire, went to the agreed spot, the parking lot of a home supply store. SOU units quickly moved into position to monitor and document the sale.

Vladimir soon arrived in the parking lot, and while looking for Bruce, he spotted an SOU van and somehow thought it was Bruce's vehicle. Warden Josh Brennan had a camcorder in hand in the front passenger seat of the van, ready to film the sale. Upon seeing Vladimir's vehicle approaching, Brennan sensed trouble and bailed the camcorder over the seatback into the rear of the vehicle, just in time. Vladimir stepped out of his Infiniti, walked over and actually opened the front passenger door of the SOU van.

"You have a sturgeon for sale?" he said.

"Huh?" said Warden Robb Allen, behind the wheel, feigning ignorance.

Vladimir slammed the door of the van and hurried back to his Infiniti. He searched further in the parking lot and soon found Bruce, who introduced himself and showed Vladimir the sturgeon.

"It's a male," said Vladimir. "And it's not cleaned. I pay $1 if not cleaned and $2 if is cleaned."

Vladimir then offered Bruce $100 for the fish, and Bruce accepted. Brennan in the SOU van filmed the transaction as Vladimir counted out five $20 bills into Bruce's hand. Bruce then helped him load the sturgeon into the trunk of the Infiniti and took advantage of the situation to ask some questions.

"How do you make caviar?" Bruce inquired.

"It very, very, very, beeg process," said Vladimir. "My mother make it."

Bruce expressed interest in seeing it done sometime, and he told Vladimir he would call him again when he had another fish. Vladimir offered some advice before he and Bruce parted company.

"No talk to anybody about this. Very, very dangerous. Fish and Game guys are buying fish on the river. Very, very dangerous. I know two guys already in jail."

Bruce agreed to be careful, then drove away, content with the knowledge that SOU, no matter what, had a piece of Vladimir, who in purchasing a sturgeon had just committed a serious violation of state law. SOU tailed Vladimir to a residence on Cedar Street in Sacramento and filmed him carrying the sturgeon into the garage. A check with DMV on the Infiniti's license number showed a registered owner of Vladimir Soltikov on Cedar Street. Vladimir's lair had now been located and his last name determined.

It was a month before SOU was able to acquire another sturgeon. Bruce immediately called Vladimir's house, and a woman answered.

"This is Troy," said Bruce. "Are you Vladimir's wife?"

"No," replied the woman. "I am Sasha, Vladimir's mother."

Troy informed her he had a sturgeon, and she immediately asked if it was male or female. He told her it was a female. She conversed briefly with someone in Russian, apparently Vladimir, then told Bruce she wanted the fish. A half hour later she met with Bruce at the parking lot of a major shopping mall. She was driving the Infiniti.

Sasha Soltikov was a squat woman with a big mouth and toad-like features. She inspected the roe of the five-foot female sturgeon.

"This no good!" she said. "Only black is good." Apparently the roe, being red and not black, was not yet mature enough for caviar, so she rejected it. But she bought the sturgeon meat, paying Bruce $60 for it. Again Bruce was wearing a wire, and SOU filmed the transaction. Sasha then drove away, unaware she was being tailed by SOU.

Sasha drove to a 7-Eleven, made a phone call, and a few minutes later an Asian male arrived in a small pickup. He immediately loaded a sturgeon from the pickup bed into the trunk of the Infiniti, and Sasha paid him in cash. SOU filmed the transaction and ran the license number. It came back to one Vang Xiong, of Sacramento.

Sasha next drove to the rear of an immigrant-owned automotive body shop, which SOU would later learn was a suspected "chop shop" for stolen cars. Vladimir was there, and wardens watched as he unloaded one of the two sturgeons and butchered it with a large knife. He carefully removed roe from the carcass, placing it into a large plastic bowl. Sasha carried the bowl into the shop, loaded the head and tail of the butchered sturgeon into the trunk of the Infiniti and drove away.

Sasha, still shadowed by an SOU tail, next went to the rear of the Good Appetite Market, an immigrant-owned food store. While SOU wardens couldn't immediately maneuver to a place from which they could view the rear of the market, they later saw and photographed a large sturgeon lying on the floor of the market, just inside the back door. The owners of the market were now in serious trouble.

The following day, an undercover warden visited the store. In the meat case, he saw what looked like sturgeon meat, but he couldn't be certain, for all of the labels were in Russian. He purchased a piece of the mystery meat, and the forensics lab, a few days later, identified it as sturgeon. The store owners were now in *more* trouble.

It was at about this time that SOU learned that Oregon State Police and the U.S. Fish and Wildlife Service were working on a sturgeon-related problem in Oregon and Washington. Columbia River sturgeon was being exploited commercially for caviar and meat. But Oregon and Washington had a very restrictive size limit on sturgeon, so it was difficult for the outlaws to get the big female Columbia River sturgeon that produced the good, black roe. California sturgeon roe was therefore being transported north to meet the considerable demand in immigrant communities in the Portland area. So, SOU began sharing notes with Oregon and the feds.

Weeks passed. The mother-and-son criminal team of Sasha and Vladimir Soltikov, monitored by SOU, continued to buy sturgeon and roe from outlaw fishermen. SOU documented these transactions and added the sellers to the growing list of suspects who would later be arrested.

Whenever the opportunity arose, Bruce sold the Soltikovs more sturgeon and sturgeon roe. Getting to know the suspects better, he learned that each of them appeared to have a drinking problem. SOU observed Vladimir one morning drunk, staggering around on his front lawn, a vodka bottle in his hand. On another occasion, both Vladimir and Sasha met with Bruce to buy a sturgeon, and both were drunk, Sasha so much so that she was dropping money all over the parking lot of a liquor store. As she argued with Bruce over the price of a fish, Bruce counted over $400 cash on the ground.

In addition to fish and roe going into the Soltikov's house, cases of canned caviar were observed going out. Tailed by SOU, Vladimir and Sasha traveled to immigrant communities all over Sacramento and sold pint Kerr jars of canned caviar. SOU identified the buyers, when possible, and added them to the list of those to be charged with the illegal buying of sport-caught sturgeon and roe.

Early in 2003, a year into the investigation, Bruce called the Soltikovs and asked them if they wanted a large sturgeon.

"It's a big one," said Bruce. "It's *too* big, 73 inches. Dangerous to transport." This was in reference to the fish's being longer than California's 72-inch maximum size limit on sturgeon.

"Only one inch too big," said Sasha, demonstrating that she was not only well aware of the legal size limits for sturgeon, but that she didn't mind buying what was obviously an illegal fish.

Bruce went to the house, sold the big fish to Sasha for $70 cash, then asked to use the bathroom. He hoped to get a look inside the house. Sasha showed Bruce into her kitchen, where he noticed they had two refrigerators. She then showed him a large bowl of caviar and the finished product in a pint-sized canning jar.

As Bruce looked on, noting four cases of pint canning jars on the floor, Sasha stirred the big bowl of caviar with a wooden spoon.

"This already cooked with rock salt, six . . . seven minutes," she said. "Then I strain it through colander."

She now added about three tablespoons of vegetable oil and stirred it into the caviar, which immediately took on a pleasing sheen.

"How do you eat it?" Bruce asked.

"With bread and butter," said Sasha.

"And vodka?" Bruce asked with a grin.

"Yes, vodka," said Sasha, giving Bruce a thumbs-up.

While at the Soltikov house, Bruce met a second man who identified himself as Nick, Vladimir's brother. SOU later ran the plates on Nick's car, and determined his real name to be Nikolai Soltikov. SOU now began surveillance on Nikolai and soon learned that he was deeply involved in the same sturgeon and caviar crimes as his brother and mother.

Following Bruce's departure, Sasha left the house with a case of caviar. SOU followed and filmed as she met three women at a gas station. She opened a bottle of caviar and allowed the women to smell it. She then put the case of caviar into the trunk of another car, and one of the women paid her in cash. SOU was later able to identify this woman through DMV, her license plate coming back to Igor and Tatyana Patrishna. Tatyana was now added to SOU's list of violators.

Weeks passed. The illegal activity continued, SOU continued to monitor it, and more suspects were added to the list. Various outlaw fishermen delivered fish and roe to Sasha and Vladimir, and to Vladimir's brother, Nikolai, at his home. Cases of canning jars went into the houses, and cases of canned caviar came out and were sold mainly in immigrant communities in Sacramento.

The Soltikovs delivered more sturgeon to the Good Appetite Market, and on one occasion, SOU filmed two women butchering three big sturgeon behind the store. The owners of the store were now in more trouble.

One afternoon, Vladimir delivered a jar of caviar to a bar and remained inside for 45 minutes. While he was inside, SOU Warden Kathy Ponting crawled under his car and attached a tracking device. Vladimir then met another man at the auto body shop, and the two of them drove to a liquor store. They purchased a bottle of vodka, walked outside and behind the store, then passed the bottle back and forth until it was empty.

When Vladimir walked unsteadily back to his car and climbed in, Ponting was faced with a dilemma. She couldn't let the man drive away drunk, and she couldn't risk blowing a yearlong investigation. She frantically radioed the sheriff's office and got lucky. A deputy sheriff was nearby and was able to get to Vladimir before he drove away. The deputy gave him a warning not to drive until he was sober and noted nine jars of caviar in the back seat. Five minutes after the deputy left, Vladimir drove away. Ponting radioed the Highway Patrol, but Vladimir parked in a strip mall before an officer could get to him.

In early February 2003, Bruce again went to Sasha and Vladimir's house. This time he brought them gifts—some canned albacore, canned asparagus and apricot jam. He told Sasha that he had a friend in Los Angeles who wanted caviar for his restaurant. He asked the price, and Sasha told him she got $50 a pint in Sacramento, but $100 in Los Angeles. But she claimed that she was out of caviar, having promised all she had to others.

As weeks passed, it became obvious to Bruce and SOU that the illegal sturgeon-related activity was increasing. The Soltikovs went to more new places to pick up sturgeon. SOU filmed them several times using a hand scale to weigh roe and paying out cash to outlaw fishermen SOU had not seen before. New players were added to the list of violators. More caviar was processed and sold by the Soltikovs. More caviar buyers were added to the list. SOU correctly concluded that they were witnessing an illegal industry that posed a grave risk to the future of California's wild sturgeon.

One night in late February, at Vladimir and Sasha's house, Ponting was on surveillance duty and saw a vehicle arrive with what appeared to be Oregon plates. Ponting immediately reached for her radio, because Oregon State Police had alerted SOU that suspects in the Portland area were planning to drive to Sacramento for a load of caviar.

As Ponting made the radio call to alert other SOU wardens, she observed a man and woman exit the car and go to the house. She then did a walk-by, confirming that the car indeed had Oregon plates. An Oregon DMV check showed the registered owners to be Yuri and Katerina Kroskov, of Portland.

Soon Vladimir and the man began loading cases of caviar into the trunk of the car. Ponting counted eight cases before the Kroskovs departed. SOU tailed them directly to Interstate 5, where they took the northbound ramp. Then began what would prove to be perhaps the longest vehicle tail in Fish and Game's history.

The Kroskovs drove straight for the Oregon border, crossing the state line at 2:40 a.m. Continuing north, they stopped for gas in Grants Pass. Hours earlier SOU had alerted the Oregon State Police to the situation and Sgt. Walt Markee, of OSP's Special Investigations Unit, and Senior Trooper Ken Snook were on hand.

Soon after the Kroskovs left Grants Pass, they found a police car behind them with emergency lights flashing. Markee and Snook were pulling them over for speeding. Snook asked for, and was granted, permission to look through the car. He soon verified the presence of eight cases of pint jars of caviar. Snook then warned the Kroskovs against speeding and sent them on their way. They continued north, driving all night.

At 7:20 a.m., they crossed the Columbia River into Washington, still tailed by the now exhausted SOU wardens. The Kroskovs then turned off Interstate 5 in Vancouver, Washington, and drove to an apartment building. Drunk with fatigue, SOU's Kathy Ponting filmed the Kroskovs' street-corner sale of 50 pounds of caviar to two men for $5000 cash. Unfortunately for the Kroskovs, the buyers were undercover agents Earl Kissler, Special Agent for U.S. Fish and Wildlife Service, and Senior Trooper Jeff Samuels of OSP.

Meanwhile, things in California continued as before with lots of buying and selling by the Soltikovs, and lots of sturgeon being slaughtered by unscrupulous outlaw fishermen. The soon-to-be-arrested list continued to grow. The question now for SOU was when to put an end to the operation.

In Vancouver, undercover agents Kissler and Samuels ordered more caviar from the Kroskovs, hoping to make another buy and bolster their case against them. In California, Bruce went to see Sasha in hopes of getting a caviar sample for a DNA comparison with the caviar purchased by the undercover agents in Vancouver. Sasha, however, had no caviar.

The caviar ordered by Kissler and Samuels from California never resulted in another covert buy, because it had apparently spoiled. Other bad luck brought the operation closer to an end. Unbeknown to SOU, the feds had been working an undercover sting on outlaw caviar dealers in Los Angeles and had made arrests. The Soltikovs apparently got wind of this, for their behavior suddenly changed. Sasha began peeking nervously out of her windows, apparently looking for surveillance people, and when Bruce took a fish to her house Vladimir slammed the door in his face.

After Bruce left, Sasha and Vladimir came out of the house, and SOU noted that Sasha had red eyes, a cut across her forehead and her arm in a cast. Vladimir went to a van parked in front, grabbed a bottle of vodka from inside and proceeded to get drunk.

All in all, it appeared that SOU's operation was outliving its effectiveness. Foley believed this to be the case, so she set her wardens to work preparing complaints against the Soltikovs and 19 other suspects.

In May of 2003, 16 months after the beginning of the sturgeon investigations, a small army of wardens descended on homes all over Sacramento. They made 10 arrests initially, and Sasha and Vladimir were grim-faced and silent as wardens placed them in handcuffs for their ride to the county jail.

Two weeks later, after the first 10 suspects had been interrogated, another small army of wardens visited more homes and arrested 12 more suspects. It would now be up to the courts.

Sasha and Vladimir ultimately pled guilty to felony conspiracy. Both were sentenced to 150 days in jail, plus fines and probation. Vladimir was fined $15,000, but the judge took pity on toad-faced Sasha, the actual ringleader, fining her only $3,000 for the same offenses. Both, however, received five years' formal probation during which time they could possess no parts of sturgeon, including roe or caviar. They were also ordered to stay clear of any waterways where sturgeon is found.

The remaining 20 suspects, most of whom pled guilty, were fined from $150 to $9,000. The outlaw fishermen among them also lost their fishing privileges for three years and were put on the same restrictive probation as the Soltikovs.

The wardens were initially annoyed over Sasha's slap on the wrist, but they felt better when they learned she was facing felony charges in Sacramento County for *grand theft* and *welfare fraud*.

The wardens also learned why they had seen her with a cut forehead and her arm in a cast. She had gotten drunk at a casino and taken a bad fall, knocking herself cold. When she awoke in an ambulance, she attacked a paramedic, striking him several times. He was not amused. So, on top of everything else, Sasha was now charged with *assault*.

***

For the game wardens, there would be one more fond memory of the Soltikovs—immigrants who had come to this country and immediately become criminals. It came about when Sasha and Vladimir arrived to reclaim their cars, which the wardens had seized into evidence at the time of their arrests.

Kathy Ponting had been given the task of returning their cars to them from an impound yard near Stockton. She was aware that both Sasha and Vladimir had suspended driver's licenses and could not legally drive. She had therefore carefully explained to them, well in advance, that they would have to bring licensed drivers with them to drive their cars away.

When the day came, however, Ponting was astounded when Sasha and Vladimir arrived alone, with Vladimir driving. Vladimir was in turn surprised when Ponting whipped out a citation book and cited him for *driving with a suspended license.*

Ponting explained to them again that neither of them was to drive. She watched as Sasha made a cell phone call for licensed drivers, three of them, to come and drive their cars home. Sasha then assured Ponting that the drivers were on their way. Ponting was reasonably certain that the "mystery drivers" would never arrive, but she didn't have time to stick around to find out. She therefore warned the two one last time against driving, then departed.

An hour later, as Ponting was heading back to Sacramento on Interstate 5 in a patrol rig, the familiar Infiniti came blasting by her with Sasha at the wheel. Ponting immediately put the red light on her and pulled her over. Sasha then sat glowering as Ponting issued *her* a citation for *driving with a suspended license.*

The Old Pro

The downed buck was all but invisible from the road, but Warden Ray Azbill spotted it instantly. A single forked antler gave it away, the tines backlit against a fast-darkening sky.

"Wait here," said Azbill as he braked the patrol pickup to a stop and threw it into park. Warden John Foster, in the passenger seat, waited obediently as Azbill leaped out, vaulted a barbed wire fence and trotted up the slope to the fallen deer. Azbill knelt beside the deer for a few seconds, his back to Foster, his hands busy at some task out of Foster's view. He then rose and hurried back down the hillside.

But as he neared the fence, a ground squirrel burrow collapsed beneath his right foot, twisting his ankle in a direction it was not meant to bend. A bolt of pain shot up his leg, and he nearly went down, but he caught himself and managed to hobble to the fence. He gingerly ducked between the barbed strands of the fence and limped back to the patrol truck.

"Wish I hadn't done *that*!" he said as he painfully climbed behind the wheel.

He drove the vehicle less than a quarter mile before turning off the road and concealing the patrol vehicle behind a large haystack.

"That deer was shot in the neck," said Azbill. "No wasted meat. Those guys will be back."

The wardens had received the call a mere 18 minutes earlier via CB radio. A rancher in a rural, mountainous part of Monterey County had heard the shot and had seen a dark blue pickup speed away. Upon investigating, the rancher had spotted the dead deer in deep grass on the hillside and had immediately tried for Azbill on the CB. Azbill had installed a CB radio in his patrol vehicle for just this reason, and as luck would have it, he and Foster were only a few miles away.

But Foster wouldn't have agreed that it was simply a matter of luck that they had been nearby, for he had learned that Azbill, something of a legend in southern Monterey County, had an uncanny ability to be in the right place at the right time. Azbill had a nose for violators, particularly night-hunting pig and deer poachers, and he loved working at night, with or without a backup warden. Over the years he had racked up a tremendous arrest record, having brought to justice hundreds of lawless scoundrels and lesser violators.

Foster, a warden of just three years' experience, was in awe of Azbill. He worked with the aging warden every chance he got, for Azbill always taught him something, a valuable bit of game warden lore or some useful trick borne of long years of hard experience. Foster greatly enjoyed the long nights spent in the hills with the old pro.

"I'll tell you what's going to happen," said Azbill, as they exited the patrol vehicle and climbed to an elevated position among the hay bales. "At around dark, the pickup will come by and drop somebody off. About 10 minutes after that, they'll come back by and pick up their drop-off *and* the deer."

If Azbill was right, the wardens wouldn't have long to wait, for the sun had already dropped behind the Coast Range mountains, and darkness would soon be upon them. Foster peered out at the meandering gravel road that began in the tiny community of Parkfield and led northeasterly through the oak woodlands hills, up and over a low range of mountains and down into the oil town of Coalinga.

It was usually wild pigs that lured poachers to this remote part of the state, but deer season had opened a week earlier, bringing more potential problems to the area. Most who came for deer were honest hunters, but some were not. In this case, it was a simple matter of two violations—*hunter trespass* and *failure to tag*. They almost certainly had committed a third violation, *shooting from a vehicle*, but the rancher had not actually witnessed this, so the wardens would not make the charge.

"I heard you caught the Sartoris again," said Foster, in reference to Azbill's capture the week before of some of the area's most infamous and dangerous outlaws. The Sartoris were a clan of low-life criminals who had terrorized Monterey County's residents for years.

"You heard right," said Azbill, as he gingerly palpated his injured ankle. "Alvin and four of the others shot a pig at around midnight about a week ago. I watched 'em do it, and I went on foot down a fence line to 'em, and it was dark enough that I got right in among them. They never noticed. I was standing there with three of 'em while Alvin and one of the others dragged the pig through the fence. I was closest to their pickup, and Alvin pointed to me and ordered me to drop the tailgate." Azbill smiled at the memory. "That's when I put the light on 'em. They were so stunned that when I ordered them to the ground, they all hit the dirt."

"You were by yourself?" Foster asked.

"By myself," said Azbill. "This makes seven times I've caught them."

Foster marveled over this amazing fact. Seven times Azbill had survived serious encounters with these aggressive, mentally unstable people. Other law enforcement agencies called out their SWAT teams when forced to deal with them.

"I'm amazed you're still alive," said Foster. "Why do you suppose they let you get away with that? Why haven't they jumped you?"

"Beats me," said Azbill. "Maybe it's because I'm not afraid of 'em."

Foster concluded that this was most likely the case, since the Sartoris were accustomed to people being terrified of them.

In the last soft glow of dusk, from a wooded draw at the far end of a meadow across from the wardens, a wild pig sow appeared, followed by a troop of half-grown piglets. The wardens watched as the sow warily led the young ones at a leisurely pace, rooting and feeding on acorns under the oaks. But suddenly the sow froze, then wheeled and ran for the wooded draw. The piglets scurried after her.

"What spooked them?" said Foster, but the sound of an approaching vehicle provided the answer.

"It's them," said Azbill. "Right on time," as a dark-colored pickup appeared, heading their way. As it reached the spot opposite the dead deer, it stopped briefly, and the wardens heard a door slam. Then it accelerated away. As it passed the haystack, its driver peered warily at the farm machinery parked there. Then it continued on.

Foster, binoculars to his eyes, felt his pulse quicken as he glimpsed a dark figure hurrying up the slope toward the deer. Then the figure vanished in the near-darkness. Both wardens now experienced the strange, but familiar, butterflies-in-the-stomach sensation that always came when action was imminent.

As though Azbill had written the script, 10 minutes later the blue pickup returned. Azbill had accurately predicted the time schedule, but the violators would now add their own twist to the scenario, for as the blue pickup reached the spot nearest the dead deer, it did not stop. It continued on up the hill and out of sight.

Almost immediately, however, a second pickup appeared, trailing the blue one, this one bright yellow. Upon reaching the spot nearest the deer, it stopped, and five seconds later the wardens heard the clatter of the tailgate dropping. Then came the clearly audible thump of a carcass landing in the steel pickup bed. Two doors now slammed and the vehicle was in motion, racing away.

The wardens clambered down from their nest among the hay bales, Azbill favoring his pain-wracked ankle. Into the patrol truck they leaped, and off they went. The engine roared and gravel flew as Azbill fishtailed them onto the roadway. Up the road they accelerated, soon reaching speeds Foster never thought he would experience on gravel. Azbill braked hard as they slid into the turns, then accelerated through them as Foster held on for his life.

As Foster experienced what he would recall as the most terrifying high-speed ride of his life, he was reminded of Azbill's driving record, which had become as legendary as the warden himself. Known for being a bit hard on equipment, Azbill had once destroyed five patrol vehicles in a single year. He had struck a cow with the first one, t-boned a car containing a drunk driver with the second, rolled his captain's sedan for number three, and demolished two others before the memorable year ended. His captain had always threatened to send him to safe driving school, but never got around to it. These thoughts coursed through Foster's terror-numbed mind until taillights appeared ahead and the overtaken vehicle yielded to Azbill's red light.

But it wasn't the yellow pickup. It was the blue one, having apparently been passed by the yellow one, and its driver stopped the vehicle dead-center in the roadway. Foster leaped out, ran forward and checked the bed of the vehicle just in case. No deer. He ran back and jumped into the patrol vehicle, but Azbill couldn't proceed, for the driver and passenger of the blue pickup had stepped out and had left their doors open, blocking the roadway. Now they were walking back, seeking conversation with the wardens.

It was clear they were attempting to delay the wardens, so Azbill shouted an unmistakable warning that sent them diving for cover as the patrol vehicle shot forward, swerved off onto the shoulder, careened around the blue pickup and tore away. Foster's wild, nightmarish ride now began anew.

Foster viewed each coming turn as potentially his last while Azbill continued his relentless, pedal-to-the-metal pursuit. But there was neither dust in the air ahead nor visible taillights. The bad guys either had a substantial lead or had turned off somewhere. The wardens could only race on and hope for the best.

They steadily gained elevation as the chase drew them northerly on the Parkfield-Coalinga Grade, the patrol vehicle hurtling through the night-darkened forest. Azbill's jaw was clenched in concentration and pain, his tortured ankle swollen double in size as he bore down upon it, alternately braking and accelerating. At last, he flung the patrol vehicle around a curve and into a long straightaway and was treated to a brief flash of red far ahead.

"We're still on 'em," he said, but Foster, braced and clinging with a death grip to whatever he could grab, offered no words of reply.

"They must really know the road," continued Azbill. "We're hardly gaining on 'em." But gaining on them they were, and the elusive taillights were in view more and more often now.

Azbill had not yet employed his red light, for no good would come from tipping his hand too early. The violators had undoubtedly seen the headlights drawing ever nearer behind them, but there was always a chance that they would think that they were being overtaken by some non-threatening driver simply driving fast, or, in this case, that they were being overtaken by their friends and accomplices in the blue pickup. Azbill would use his red light, and possibly the siren, only to make the stop.

The violators had indeed been fooled. This became apparent when the wardens reached the Monterey-Fresno County line, which followed the summit of a long ridge that separated the arid country of the San Joaquin Valley to the east from the green, forested hills of the coastal mountains to the west. When the wardens reached the ridgetop, Azbill pulled to a sliding stop, for he had a good view of the road descending toward Coalinga, and he saw neither taillights nor the glow of headlights. Had the violators turned off? Azbill killed the engine to listen.

Silence prevailed for only a few seconds before a horn honked surprisingly close by. The attention of the wardens was drawn to an old spur road that left the main road a mere 60 yards behind the patrol vehicle. Azbill fired the engine, spun a U-turn and plunged down the spur road. The patrol vehicle's high-beams immediately illuminated the yellow pickup which contained two half-blinded deer poachers.

Azbill switched on his red light and with the powerful beam of his overhead spotlight, further illuminated the interior of the vehicle. Foster had stepped out, and Azbill now did the same. They carefully moved forward, flashlights in their left hands, gun hands on their pistol butts.

"State game wardens, men!" said Azbill in a firm voice. "Get your hands up where we can see 'em!"

The two suspects complied, raising their hands.

"Now, could you very slowly step out, please?" While Azbill phrased it as a request, the tone of his voice left no doubt that it was a command.

Both men stepped out, hands still raised. Azbill directed his man, the passenger, to face away, and he handcuffed him. Foster followed Azbill's lead, handcuffing the driver. For Azbill, this precaution was borne of hundreds of night stops involving armed violators. Handcuffing the violators, at least initially, provided the wardens a great margin of safety, and Azbill had learned that while the violators were suffering their initial shock at being caught, there was a narrow window of opportunity when they could often be rather easily handcuffed. Later, when the shock began to wear off, they often became belligerent and uncooperative, and the wardens were more likely to have a fight on their hands.

Foster walked back and flashed his light in the bed of the violators' pickup. The dead buck was there, its big eyes still bright and shining.

During the investigation that followed, the driver admitted to shooting the deer, but he claimed that he had shot it legally on public land. The passenger denied any involvement in the incident, claiming he had not touched the deer or assisted in any way.

"Then how did you get blood on your pants?" said Azbill, pointing out the fresh crimson smears on the man's Levi's.

"I . . . er . . . uh," the man stammered, but he came up with no plausible explanation.

As for the driver's claim that he had legally killed the deer on public hunting land, Azbill was able to deftly put this claim to rest as well. But he was never able to get them to identify their accomplices in the blue pickup. Nor would they explain anything about their mysterious transfer from one vehicle to another. These things were to remain a mystery.

The wardens, however, knew all they needed to make a good case against the two men for their illegal killing of a deer on private land that was fenced and heavily posted *NO HUNTING OR TRESPASSING*. And there was, of course, the matter of the deer being untagged, an additional violation. The wardens transferred the deer to the back of the patrol vehicle, then issued citations to both suspects, removing their handcuffs so they could sign their names in the appropriate boxes. Soon thereafter, the wardens completed their business and sent the two deer poachers on their way.

Foster drove the patrol vehicle on the ride back toward Parkfield, Azbill having done all the driving he intended to do that night with his injured ankle. They searched for the blue pickup and the two accomplices but never saw them again. The following day, an X-ray of Azbill's ankle would reveal that he had fractured it in two places.

In the end, both of the poachers felt they had no chance to prevail in court, so they forfeited bail. They were sickened as they left the courthouse that day, each having parted with about two weeks' pay.

Strangely enough, it later came to Azbill's attention that the two men were spreading a bogus story about their arrests. In fact, a friend of Azbill's, a Coalinga resident, asked Azbill about the arrests, claiming that the two suspects were telling people that the judge had let them off with no fines and that the wardens, at the time of the arrest, had been afraid of them.

To this, Azbill laughed and said, "Ask them if the wardens were so afraid of them, how were they able to send one of them home without his pants." This was in reference to Azbill's decision to seize the passenger's bloodstained pants into evidence.

"Here's the problem," Azbill had told the man. "I need your pants for evidence. Now, I can take you 70 miles to the county jail in Monterey and get you a pair of orange jail pants, or I can send you home from here in your shorts. It's your choice." The man had chosen the second option and had ridden back to Coalinga in his undershorts.

Foster had been amused by all of this at the time of the arrests, but he had learned a thing or two as well. For one thing, he had learned to admire Azbill's easy, respectful demeanor while dealing with captured violators. Azbill had the remarkable ability to leave violators feeling not that he had brought them to grief, but feeling as though he had somehow done them a service. They often, in fact, thanked him when he left them.

Of the lessons Foster had learned that night, he would certainly never forget the way Azbill had destroyed the driver's fictional defense story that he had killed the deer legally on public land. Azbill had set a trap for the man, and when it happened, Foster was reminded of the brief seconds Azbill had been alone with the deer on the rancher's hillside, just before he injured his ankle.

When Azbill sprang his trap, he summoned both handcuffed violators to the right side of the yellow pickup, where the dead deer lay in the bed. While Foster illuminated Azbill and the deer with his flashlight, Azbill faced the violators.

"Watch me," he told them. Then he held his hands up and turned them first one way and then the other, like a magician.

"Nothing in my hands," he said as he did so.

Then he grasped first the left sleeve of his short-sleeve uniform shirt, then the right, holding the sleeves briefly open.

"Nothing up my sleeves," he said as he did so.

Then, with something of a flourish, he reached with two fingers into the half-open mouth of the dead buck and withdrew a bloody rectangle of stiff paper.

Raymond Azbill, it read, *Fish and Game Warden.*

"Do you suppose this deer was eating my business card when you shot him?" Azbill inquired.

To this, the suspects had no reply.

Zero Choice

A still October night in the forest.

The green patrol vehicle, a four-by-four pickup, was all but invisible in the darkness. Alert behind the wheel, Warden Josh Brennan, California Department of Fish and Game, peered down into the dark void that was the Feather River Canyon. Deer season was open, and Brennan knew that it was a good night for frustrated hunters to illegally spotlight a buck. So he was there to remind them of the law.

He had chosen a high point, a log landing off Big Bend Road, a place that overlooked the canyon and the Feather River below. To the east he could see roughly two miles of Bardees Bar Road, with its many switchbacks, as it descended into the canyon. The log landing was a good perch from which to watch for outlaws, but he knew his chances for encountering spotlighters in the vast forests of the Sierra Nevada were never good. But Brennan would put in the time, for he was a pro, one of the relatively few wardens who routinely worked alone at night, one of the few with the courage to face armed violators in remote places with no hope for timely backup.

But luck was with him on this night, for a slow-moving vehicle appeared on Bardees Bar Road an hour before midnight. Brennan studied it through his binoculars. It was a quad-runner all-terrain vehicle carrying two suspects, the passenger actively shining a powerful hand-held spotlight first one way then the other, obviously searching for deer. Brennan watched as the suspects traveled to the bottom of the canyon and were out of sight for a while. Then he saw them again, apparently returning. They had not gone far when they stopped, their spotlight trained on something he could not see. Then two loud shots rang out, echoing off the canyon walls. Seconds later the quad-runner was moving again, traveling fast with just headlight and taillights. This in no way surprised Brennan, who correctly concluded that the suspects were in a hurry to get clear of the area and to stash any guns they had. He believed they had shot a deer and would return for it later. So, he remained where he was as they drove out of the canyon and away.

It was during the two hours that followed that something unexpected happened. Vehicle lights appeared on the same road between Brennan and the river. He watched as it continued all the way to the canyon floor and then out onto a gravel bar near the river. Then the headlights went out. He reached for his binoculars and focused on the spot, but he could see nothing.

Several minutes passed then suddenly he was startled by a brilliant flash of light there, light that illuminated the whole gravel bar and much of the lower canyon. Throwing his binoculars to his eyes, Brennan saw a large pile of trash ablaze near a pickup truck. He recognized the truck immediately, a large newer model Ford F-250 diesel painted entirely in camo. Standing beside the vehicle, and also clearly visible, was the pickup's owner, one Clinton Bates, a local dope grower. Brennan had encountered him on the road a few times, once just a week earlier. Due to recent changes in California law, the wardens now turned a blind eye to small-scale marijuana growing as long as the growers did not harm wildlife. Brennan had reminded Bates of this unwritten understanding, and Bates assured Brennan that he was well aware of it.

Brennan, despite his anger at seeing a pickup load of trash dumped by the river, drenched in gasoline and ignited, resisted the urge to immediately pounce on Bates. But he knew where Bates was camped in an old motorhome near his grow, so there was no urgency. He could deal with Bates the following day. It proved to be a good decision, for an hour later, the spotlighting suspects again appeared on the quad-runner, driving down into the canyon. Brennan watched as they traveled along, and soon the spotlight came on again. When they reached the area where the shots had been fired, they stopped and turned off their lights. Twenty minutes later, their lights came on again and Brennan watched them driving his way again. A few minutes later, the suspects rounded a tight turn and were suddenly nose to nose with Brennan's patrol rig and drenched in bright emergency lights. They skidded to a stop and sat as though petrified.

"State game warden," announced Brennan, advancing with a bright flashlight held high in his left hand, his right hand near his holstered Glock sidearm. "Turn off your engine and keep your hands where I can see them." As he approached, Brennan noticed a small buck deer lashed to the rear cargo carrier of the ATV.

The suspects were cooperative, and Brennan was quick to note that the driver appeared to be intoxicated, finding it difficult to stand. But he would not be driving again that night, for Brennan, upon running their names through dispatch, learned of a warrant out for the driver's arrest. He also discovered a semiautomatic pistol stuffed in the driver's waistband. All of this added up to a free ride for the driver, securely handcuffed, to county jail. Brennan cited and released the second suspect and sent him on his way. He then hefted the evidence deer into the back of his patrol rig and departed.

***

It was well after 3:00 a.m. when Brennan made it home. He thankfully crawled into bed, but as usual, it would be but a brief night's sleep. His wife, Elaine, the perfect game warden wife, always believed he deserved as much sleep as possible after working long nights. But his daughter, Rachael, age three, disagreed. Brennan found himself jarred awake shortly after 7:00.

Brennan had not intended to work on this day, for it was October eighth. Six years earlier on this date, he had married Elaine, a choice he considered one of the best of his life. Over the years he had tried to take that special day off when possible, but he would be spending his anniversary morning this year writing his report on his spotlighting arrests of the night before. He had related to Elaine his observation of Bates, the pot grower, and the man's particularly disgusting trash-dumping violation. He then explained his need to follow up. He told Elaine that he would be gone for only a couple of hours, and he would be home in plenty of time to take her out to dinner.

"You'll be home for dinner?" she said with a twinkle in her eye. "I've heard that before." It was something of a joke between them, for she had been married to a game warden far too long to believe her warden husband when he told her he would be home for dinner.

"Well, this time I'll be home," he replied.

But he was wrong.

He could feel fall in the air as he descended Bardees Bar Road to the river bar below, and what he found there disturbed him. What had been a heaping pickup load of trash and garbage dumped there by Bates the night before was still smoking, only partially burned. There were old paint cans, propane bottles, household chemicals, rodent poison, fertilizer bags, food wrappers and bags of household trash and garbage. On top of it all were the smoldering remains of a recliner. Brennan was disgusted. After thoroughly photographing the dump, he headed back up the canyon.

He passed the locked gate to Bates' steep, roughly graded driveway, continuing on to a high place where he knew his radio would work. He called dispatch and advised them of his location, and advised them he would be citing Clinton Bates for his misdeeds. He then turned around and drove back down to the locked gate. He parked there and hiked up the driveway.

It was a steep, 100-yard grade to the log landing on which sat two vehicles. When they first came into view, Brennan noted that both were parked against the steep cut bank on the upslope side of the landing. The big Ford camo pickup was parked immediately ahead of a medium-sized motorhome. Bates was busy between the two vehicles and a man Brennan knew only as "Crowder" was at work, standing in the bed of the pickup. Both were wiry-looking, sun-tanned men in their early thirties. Bates, medium height, looked like a surfer with shoulder-length sun-bleached hair. As soon as Brennan saw them, he called out to them.

"Fish and Game, men." Startled, the two men froze and stared at the warden. "Mr. Bates," said Brennan. "I need to talk to you."

Brennan got Bates aside and informed him that he had seen him dump trash by the river and set it on fire. He further explained that it was against state law to deposit trash or litter within 150 yards of state waters.

"I'm sorry, man," said Bates, hanging his head. "I'm really sorry." He was calm and soft-spoken. Brennan explained to him that he, Bates, would have to accompany him down to the patrol vehicle where he would be issued a citation. Bates complied, appearing genuinely ashamed of himself. Brennan wrote the citation, and Bates signed it and accepted his copy. Bates then did something unexpected. He held out his right hand. Brennan regarded the grimy hand, then reluctantly gave it a shake.

Upon leaving Bates, Brennan drove up to the high spot where he had earlier radioed dispatch. He now called dispatch again, provided them with Bates' full name and asking them to run the man for warrants. Brennan soon learned that Bates was a fugitive, wanted in Hawaii for violating parole. Not only was there a felony warrant out for him, but Hawaiian authorities were eager to fly to the mainland and pick him up.

Brennan was about to request backup for the felony arrest, but hesitated. It would take most of an hour for backup to get to him, and he was in a hurry to get home. Besides, he thought, he had just left Bates. The man had been completely mellow and cooperative. So, he decided to make the arrest on his own, as he was well accustomed to doing.

Again Brennan parked by the locked gate, and again he hiked up the steep driveway. What he saw first, upon reaching the landing, was Crowder, still standing in the pickup bed, but now he was holding a huge pipe wrench the length of his arm. Bates, standing by the pickup's passenger door, looked up, spotted Brennan, and was not happy to see him.

"Mr. Bates. There's a warrant out for your arrest," said Brennan. "I'm gonna have to take you in."

Bates just stood there for a moment, then began to hyperventilate, a wild and desperate look coming over him.

"Turn around and put your hands behind your back," said Brennan, taking a step toward him.

At this, Bates, looking like he would explode, blurted out, "I need a drink," and in an instant, he turned, jerked open the pickup's door and grabbed for something inside.

"Don't," shouted Brennan, certain he was going for a gun. Brennan went for his sidearm, but Bates emerged almost instantly, not with a gun, but with a juice box, one of the small cardboard drinking containers children carry in lunch boxes. With trembling hands, Bates ripped the tiny drinking straw from the side of the box, jammed it through the foil opening in the top, and with eyes bulging, he sucked mightily on the straw, draining the box in less than three seconds. Tossing it aside, he walked in tight circles for a few seconds, ignoring commands from Brennan. Then suddenly he sprinted for the motorhome. Brennan shouted for him to stop, but Bates threw open the side door on the motorhome and dove inside.

Brennan pulled his handset radio from his belt and spoke urgently into it, calling for backup. As he did so, he backed away from the vehicles so that he could see both the motorhome door and Crowder, who was looking on in astonishment. He jammed his radio back into the carrier on his belt and reached for his gun. He had no sooner begun his draw, when Bates jumped out the door with a shotgun.

"Drop it," shouted Brennan, but it was too late. Bates, partially hidden behind the open door, was swinging the shotgun barrel toward Brennan when Brennan fired four quick shots.

Bates staggered and went down onto all fours, losing the shotgun which landed a few feet from him. He began crawling toward the shotgun, a torrent of blood gushing from a terrible wound in his neck. Brennan shouted for him to stop and get on the ground, but Bates again ignored him. Bates grabbed the shotgun and was turning with it when Brennan fired again. Bates collapsed on top of the shotgun and lay still in a pool of blood.

Brennan stood for a few seconds, stunned by the enormity of what had happened. A man lay bleeding, and he had just survived a gunfight by the narrowest of margins. He sucked in great draughts of air as it all sunk in. He then turned to Crowder and said, incredulously, "Did you see that? What was he doing?"

"Don't know," said Crowder, "But I know what he's doin' now. He's dyin'."

***

Within a few hours of the shooting, Brennan was the subject of an officer-involved shooting investigation. Butte County's task force for this purpose had rented two adjoining rooms at Holiday Inn Express in Oroville, the county seat. Brennan went into one room, and witness Crowder was taken into the other. It was there that Brennan was asked to turn over his gun. Immediately after he handed over his sidearm, they provided him an identical loaner gun to temporarily replace it. Then Brennan met with his attorney, who had traveled there from Sacramento.

Upon leaving the motel, Brennan went to the District Attorney's office. It was there that he was encouraged to tell his story. Then came a careful reconstruction of the violent events of the day, and Brennan was impressed at how thoroughly and respectfully he was questioned. When coaxed through his memories of the actual shooting, he recalled something that had probably saved his life. When Bates first burst from the motorhome with the shotgun, the man was attempting to pump the shotgun, to jack a shell into the firing chamber. But the shotgun wouldn't cycle because there was a shell already in the chamber. The shotgun was ready to fire. It was the half second it took Bates to realize this that allowed Brennan to complete his draw and bring his Glock sidearm into play before Bates could fire.

Brennan would learn that his first round went through the motorhome door, ripped through Bates' left hand, continued through the shotgun stock, then bounced harmlessly off his chest, its energy spent. The second shot sent a hollow-point bullet through Bates' neck, demolishing at least one of his carotid arteries. The third shot went through the door, just above his head. The fourth shot missed entirely. The last shot, when Bates was on the ground, again trying to point the shotgun at Brennan, ripped through his heart.

Following the questioning, Brennan waited in another room for a short time, then Mike Ramsey, the district attorney of Butte County, joined him. Ramsey, an aggressive, well-respected prosecutor and master of his trade, informed him that the shooting was clearly justified, and that Crowder, the only witness, had fully corroborated Brennan's account of the incident.

"Unless some new evidence falls from the stars, you're in the clear," said Ramsey. But Ramsey, out of concern that Crowder might be encouraged to reconsider his testimony, had seen to it that Crowder, with a one-way ticket, was soon on a jet bound for Hawaii.

On the day of the shooting, Elaine Brennan returned from an overnight visit with her sister in the Bay Area. When she arrived home that afternoon, she found a nice bouquet of flowers with a note from her husband wishing her a happy anniversary. Then she was stunned by a call from Lt. Kent Harrison, a Fish and Game friend of theirs. Harrison broke the news to her that Josh was okay, but that he had been involved in a fatal shooting. A short time later, Elaine received another call from a Fish and Game employee, this one scaring her by offering to have a female officer come and sit with her. "Is he alright or isn't he?" she asked, much distressed. The caller quickly assured her that her husband was safe and uninjured. But now Elaine urgently needed to talk to her husband. It wasn't until after midnight that he finally walked through the door.

It's a well-known fact that officers involved in fatal shootings have notoriously bad memories of exactly how the shootings went down. It's like their brains go into slow motion, and they only remember bits and pieces of what occurred. For instance, an officer who claims with certainty that he only fired twice is astonished to learn later that investigators on the scene recovered eight of his fired shell casings. It's therefore not surprising that there were differences in the way Brennan and

Crowder remembered what happened that day. The most surprising difference was that Crowder remembered Bates actually firing the shotgun at Brennan, while Brennan had no memory of that whatsoever. The shotgun, found beneath Bates' body, had a live round in the chamber and the safety was in the "off" position. The four-round magazine contained only three rounds, and there were numerous fired shotgun empties scattered over the landing. It's quite possible that Bates fired prematurely when he came out of the motorhome, then pumped another round into the firing chamber an instant before Brennan fired at him.

It's also well known that officers involved in fatal shootings often deny that they have been emotionally affected by it, and they resist counseling. While they truly believe this to be true, it most often is not. Almost all such officers suffer at least some level of PTSD. In Brennan's case, for several months following the shooting he experienced unreasonable anger over small annoyances. He and Elaine would also find that he had problems watching movies containing bloody shooting scenes. At first, Brennan would simply get up and walk away. Later, however, he discouraged his family from watching such movies in his home.

Brennan is a genuine tough guy with remarkable courage, and he handled the disturbing incident well. Many officers would have been forever haunted by it or even destroyed by it, but Brennan felt only anger toward Bates for making it happen. The man had done his best to leave Elaine Brennan a widow and little Rachael fatherless, and Brennan experienced no guilt whatsoever over what he had been forced to do.

But there was one sad aftereffect that would always remain with Brennan. His close brush with death had taken some of the enjoyment out of the job he loved, and from that day forward he was no longer the fearless swashbuckler of a game warden he had been before. His grim reminder of the tenuous nature of his existence had changed him, left him far more cautious, and the job became far less fun.

A few months following the shooting, little Rachael Brennan celebrated her fourth birthday. Her father was in attendance on that day . . . and he was particularly grateful to be there.

***

Author's note: Several decades ago, I learned that a young boy, age 11, was reading my books and had decided that he wanted to become a game warden when he grew up. I signed a book for him then, including the words, "I hope someday that you will be a game warden." He never gave up on his dream, and not only did he become a warden, he ultimately became one of the absolute best wardens I have ever known. His name? Josh Brennan.

> These last three stories (*Death on Snake Mountain, Confession, Heartless Bastard*) first appeared in the magazine,
> **INTERNATIONAL GAME WARDEN.**
> These rare, first-person accounts of events were experienced by the author himself.

DEATH ON SNAKE MOUNTAIN

The smell of death was suddenly upon me. It's a bad memory you don't forget, the revolting stench of decaying human flesh, and I knew it well. I was still driving when it struck me like a physical blow, a full 100 yards downwind of my destination, the isolated home on the forested slopes of Snake Mountain. With a deep feeling of foreboding, I had to steel myself for what I knew lay ahead for me on that dark night.

The call had come in just before midnight, and the events that followed would prove to be among the most disturbing of my career. I was in a small plane at the time, high over the vast forests of eastern Butte County, searching for bad guys. Wardens on the ground were strategically positioned, primed for action, ready to pounce on any wildlife-abusing outlaws I might spot from the air. It was a Butte County Sheriff's dispatcher who put out the call for any Fish and Game unit near Oroville, a small town in the Sierra Nevada foothills.

"Butte County, go ahead to Fish and Game two-one-eleven," came the voice of Leonard Blissenbach, one of the wardens I supervised. The dispatcher then requested that he respond to a remote residence on Snake Mountain, about a 45 minute drive above Oroville.

"Our deputies are there, investigating a possible homicide," continued the dispatcher. "But they believe the house to be full of live rattlesnakes, and they're requesting a warden to clear the house for them before they go in."

As I digested this unusual information, I realized that Blissenbach had yet to answer. It was as though he had lost his voice. Then I remembered why. Blissenbach had a small problem. While he was absolutely fearless when it came to dealing with all manner of criminals and the armed hillbillies-with-attitudes we chased around, an encounter with a snake could turn him to jelly. It was a deep-seated fear so intense that if some foolish prankster were to tease him with a live snake, Blissenbach would likely kill him. Because the other wardens were too far away, I chose to spare Blissenbach embarrassment and take the call myself. Within a half hour I was back on the ground in my patrol rig, racing for Snake Mountain.

As I said, I could smell the dead body well before I reached the house. I was greeted by nervous deputies who told me the story. The occupant of the house, a middle-aged man, was a herpetologist who specialized in rattlesnakes. The man's brother, who had not heard from him in a while and could not reach him by phone, had decided to go check on him. The brother had arrived at the house that morning, and upon opening the front door had recoiled in total horror. The stench had nearly taken him to his knees, and there were live rattlesnakes almost at his feet. He bolted away, badly shaken, and for reasons unknown did not notify authorities until late that night.

When he finally spoke to deputies, he explained that his brother had devoted his two-bedroom house to the care and feeding of his huge collection of rattlesnakes in terrariums. Although no deputies had entered the house, they had observed, through the open front door, that the front glass of every terrarium they could see had been shattered and pushed in by somebody, apparently to free the snakes.

Because the house was a possible crime scene, I was asked to disturb nothing unless it could conceal a rattlesnake. And so it was that I entered the house of horrors that night, gagging from the overpowering stench, longing for a cigar or a bottle of Vicks. The place was badly cluttered, and I was amazed at the number of lighted terrariums. They were everywhere, on shelves on every wall I could see, three rows high. Each contained sand and a plastic igloo-like shelter. All had been destroyed, the front glass smashed in, and I saw no snakes in any of them.

On the living room couch, I found the dead man, a seething mass of corruption. I would later learn that he had been dead for over two weeks. He was stretched out on his back, ankles crossed, his left arm extended horizontally into the room as though pointing at something. A wriggling procession of maggots were falling one by one off the tip of his index finger. As I stood there, on the verge of retching, I spotted the apparent cause of death, a plastic bag over his head. But I also noted a baseball bat on the floor near the couch. Suicide? Or did he have help? Not my problem.

I shouted information to the waiting deputies, my observations concerning the dead body. I then did a quick, but careful, walk-through of the rest of the house, snapping on all lights, expecting to see snakes in every corner.

Only one room, a bedroom, contained no terrariums, but was crammed instead with wire cages on tables and benches. On the floor were large sacks of rodent food. The room was obviously dedicated to the propagation of rodents, obviously to feed the snakes. The doors on all of the cages stood open, and the food sacks on the floor appeared to have been torn open and ravaged by hundreds of rats and mice. It appeared that they, like the snakes, had been intentionally released. This brought to my mind a nightmare vision of the dead man on the couch with a hundred or more loose rattlesnakes on the floor around him, pursuing a thousand or more loose rats and mice.

To this point, I had seen nothing alive in the house, no snakes, no rodents. So now I began a thorough room by room, nerve-jangling search on hands and knees. With flashlight and improvised snake hook in hand, I cautiously crawled through the entire house, peering under every piece of furniture including the couch bearing the dead body. I opened all low cupboards and drawers, searched boxes of junk, squinted into every possible container and stirred through piles of cast-off clothing. I expected at any second to encounter a disturbed rattlesnake coiled to strike.

I would love to tell you that I strode through the house, fearlessly stuffing scores of venomous reptiles into pillow cases, but it didn't happen. I found not one rattlesnake and not a single rat or mouse. Apparently, during the 12 or so hours the front door had stood open the previous day, everything alive in the house had gladly escaped and gone elsewhere.

It wasn't until I stood up, my search ended, that I spotted a single terrarium with the glass front still intact. The glass had been shattered, but it had somehow held together. I slid back the top to this terrarium and carefully lifted the plastic igloo. Beneath it, comfortably coiled, regarding me with its serpent eyes, was a beautiful rattlesnake. It was about a two-footer, a lovely shade of pink.

Before I left the house that night, I took a last sad look at the remains of the man on the couch. Why had he chosen to end his life? Was he terminally ill? Was he in pain? Unending depression maybe? Whatever it was, visiting the scene of his death had left me with disturbing thoughts, for I knew what he had done. Upon making his final decision to end it all, he had grabbed a baseball bat and made one last tour of his house, bashing in the terrarium fronts, freeing the snakes that he loved. He had also walked through the rodent room and opened all of the cage doors, releasing the rats and mice. He had then returned to the living room, reclined on the couch, pulled the plastic bag over his head and suffocated himself.

It took over a month to get the dead-man smell out of my mind, to not think about it, to not believe that it had somehow become a permanent part of me. Although my wife could smell nothing, it was real to me, seeming to cling to my brain. Actually, it never did fully leave me. As I write this, 20 years later, the indescribable stench of that horrible night revisits me as though it were yesterday.

***

So now, after struggling through this grisly tale, if any of you have an "Aw, that's nothin', you should hear what happened to me" story, please call me and I'll write it up.

Confession

I once tried to kill a man. I pulled my sidearm, aimed it straight at an outlaw duck hunter's chest and pulled the trigger. The dark memory of this incident has weighed heavily on me for over 45 years.

It was January, 1974, and I'd been a warden for just over a year. I was working late-shooting waterfowl hunters in the Sacramento/San Joaquin Delta, a vast and confusing expanse of islands and twisting waterways over 40 miles across. The problem was a small, uninhabited island, Little Frank's Tract, that was about a quarter mile long and half that distance across. Like many islands in the Delta, Little Frank's had a 10-foot-tall rock levee with a road on top around it, built by our government during the 1930s. Over the years, some of the Delta levees had failed during bad winters, flooding their island's interiors. Some of these were repaired, the islands pumped out. Some were left as they were.

Such was the case with Little Frank's Tract. It remained flooded, and at some point was designated a state park. As a state park, it couldn't be hunted, and ducks, as they somehow do, figured this out and congregated there during duck season by the tens of thousands. They would spend their days in safety on the island, then fly off in vast flocks at dusk to forage elsewhere. Hunters in boats along the edge of the island could often pick off a low-flying duck or two just at the end of legal shooting time. The less honorable among these hunters would stay longer and kill limits or even more.

I had discovered this enforcement problem a year earlier when I was just days out of the police academy. My captain had given me a tour of my new patrol area and had shown me the 16-foot, inboard/outboard skiff that went with it. The skiff was tied up at a boat marina on Bethel Island, at the edge of the Delta. I had returned for a closer look at my skiff an evening or two later, and it was then that I heard distant shotgun fire. A glance at my watch proved that it was just after the close of legal shooting hours. I stood for a while and listened. The shooting continued.

I grabbed some gear from my patrol rig and hurried back to the skiff. The hidden key was where it was supposed to be and the fuel tank was full. The engine started easily, and with no idea whatsoever as to where I was going, I headed out. The afterglow of sunset provided a directional reference, so I threaded my way through a confusing maze of islands, stopping once or twice until I heard more shooting. Then, when I realized that a strong current was taking me in the right direction, I cut the engine and drifted.

It was not quite dark when I watched through my binoculars as two men in a boat clearly shot at ducks. I fired the engine, drove to them and issued two of my very first citations. When the late-shooters were gone, I lingered there for a short time, exhilarated, listening to the wondrous cacophony of a night sky filled with waterfowl, amazed at my good fortune of having become a game warden.

Then reality struck me. I had no idea how to get back to Bethel Island and my boat slip. I was totally lost. But I knew which way the violators had gone, so I raced off in that direction, a rising moon lighting the way. Soon I rounded a turn and spotted them ahead. I slowed down and followed them back to the very marina where my boat slip awaited me. What a fine end to a fine day and a grand adventure.

So, a year later and a lot smarter, I was at the same place where I had caught my first late-shooters, Little Frank's Tract. I had made more arrests there during preceding evenings and had been frustrated by the fact that there were always several boats, usually at least 100 yards apart, anchored a few feet from the island with hunters shooting late. The problem was that by the time I wrote citations and finished with the first violators, the others had departed. So, I had come up with a plan to do better.

Arriving early on this evening, I hid my boat on the far side of the island and hiked 15 minutes to where things would happen. My plan was to get close to a boat, watch them shoot late, then step out and identify myself. I would order them to come to me, collect identification from them, order them to stay put, then hurry on foot to the next violators. I thought I could at least double my effectiveness. Why take singles when you can flock shoot 'em, right?

The bad guys showed up that night right on time, and I was there, the fox in the henhouse. I sneaked up on my first customers, two guys in an outboard-powered skiff anchored about 10 feet from the levee. There were plenty of willows and blackberries on the levee to conceal me, so I got close, looking right down their throats. Soon they both shot at ducks, 12 minutes after legal shooting time. Three birds fell, and a drake pintail landed no more than six feet from me. Had I been smart, I would have simply waited for them to finish their illegal shoot and come ashore to retrieve their ducks. I could have then pounced on them. But, as I said, I had become greedy, intent on getting to other violators shooting farther down the levee.

So, I chose that moment to act, stepping into view in full uniform, no more than seven yards from them.

"Good evening, gentlemen. State game warden," I announced. "I'll have to ask you to come over to me."

They blinked in surprise for a few seconds, then the guy in front untied the anchor line and spoke under his breath to the man in back. Suddenly the guy in the back of the boat reached for the pull cord on the outboard motor. The guy in the front tossed the anchor line overboard, stood up with his shotgun and aimed it directly at my face. Fortunately I was ready. I had unsnapped my holster before showing myself, and my gun-hand was on the grips of my revolver. When I saw the man's shotgun coming up, I simultaneously drew the revolver and threw myself hard to the left, certain I was about to be shot. As I hit the ground, I aimed for the man's chest and pulled the trigger.

So, you might ask, how could I get off an accurate shot under such circumstances? Well, I had been a pistol shooter all of my adult life and had competed in pistol matches in the military. I had a knack for it and would later compete at the highest levels of police combat pistol competitions. But some good luck came into play on this evening as well. When I hit the ground on my left side, arms extended, my revolver in a two-handed grip, the gun miraculously was pointed right at the guy no more than 20 feet away. I hardly had to adjust my aim as I pulled the trigger.

Before I continue with my story, I must digress a bit. Earlier that same year, my department had decided to provide their game wardens with sidearms. Before that, we had supplied our own. I had purchased a Smith & Wesson, Model 19, .357 Magnum revolver with a 6-inch barrel. I loved that gun. It would have been a great choice at the time for our department-furnished sidearms, but my department went a different direction. They purchased .357 Magnum revolvers made by Dan Wesson. These weapons offered some interesting advantages. You could, for instance, change barrels. With four barrel choices, you could exchange your long barrel for a snubby if the need arose or any other combination of gun and barrel. And the Dan Wessons were cheaper than the Smiths. But with their advantages came one glaring disadvantage. They sometimes wouldn't shoot. The hammer would fall, but the round would somehow not fire.

When we wardens first brought this deficiency to the attention of the department brass, we were told to keep carrying and shooting the guns in hopes that they would break in and become more reliable. Besides, as they reminded us, the guns shot most of the time. We were all outraged, and I, being a more serious shooter than most, put a lot of rounds through mine and determined that it misfired about one in seven shots. As fate would have it, I was wearing this defective Dan Wesson revolver the night I found myself peering down the cavernous bore of an outlaw's 12 gage shotgun.

As the action went down that evening on Little Frank's Tract, it happened in slow motion for me. In truth, the whole incident probably took place in little more than two seconds. When I pulled the trigger, my Dan Wesson went "click" instead of "boom." At that instant, the bad guy lost his balance and plopped down in the seat, his shotgun no longer trained on me. As I began my pull for a second try, I realized that the boat was in motion and the guy was no longer a threat to me. It would have been wrong for me to shoot him then, but I just couldn't let him drive away. He was in my sights, as good as dead, for I had never known the Dan Wesson to misfire twice in a row. But at the last millisecond, I altered my aim slightly and pulled the trigger again. This time the gun fired, and I put a .357 Magnum bullet through his outboard motor. It made a wonderful clanging sound, but the engine continued running and the bad guys made good their escape.

Rising to my feet again, I stood for a bit, pondering the enormity of what had just happened. I had nearly killed a man, just a year into my career. But worse, I had intentionally shot a hole through an outboard motor just inches from the relatively innocent man running it. I was suddenly terrified, certain that I would be fired from the job I had loved from the moment I first pulled on the uniform.

As I stood there, in utter despair, it dawned on me that the only witnesses to my poor judgement were unlikely to report it. So, when I wrote the story in my report that night, I didn't actually lie to my captain, one of the best men I had ever known, I simply left a little bit out. Why put him in the sad position of having to fire such an enthusiastic subordinate as me? Anyway, that was my rationalization at the time.

My captain is now dead and gone, a man I would have gladly have taken a bullet for. So now, after suffering 45 years of guilt over deceiving him, it's finally off my chest. I feel unburdened, a vast relief. I'm sure my old department will be outraged upon learning of this, but as for them, they'll have to rehire me to fire me.

Heartless Bastard

John "Shorty" McHugh had no legs. The first time I saw him, he was by himself, launching a boat in the Feather River. It was his equipment that first caught my eye, his beautiful new ¾ ton, 4X4 pickup and his magnificent 20-foot jet boat. He had already prepared the boat for launch, for without hesitation he expertly backed the boat and trailer down the ramp and into the water with a splash. The boat slid free, floating away from the trailer, attached to it by a 30-foot rope.

The door of the pickup then sprang open and out he swung, immediately capturing my complete attention. From his waist up, he was muscled like an NFL linebacker, but his legs were missing below mid-thigh. Upon reaching the ground, he launched himself down the ramp, flinging himself along with his long arms and leg-stumps in a primitive, ape-like gait that made the hair on the back of my neck prickle. Upon reaching the trailer, he untied the rope, pulled in the boat and tied it to a tree. He then scuttled back to his specially equipped pickup, scrambled up and into the driver's seat, then drove up and parked in a parking area. He soon returned on foot, so to speak, propelling himself along faster than most men can walk. I was amazed, having never seen a seriously handicapped person appear less handicapped. He untied the boat, rolled into it, fired the engine, threw it into reverse and backed away from the beach. Swinging it around, he jammed the throttle forward and shot away upstream, toward the river's infamous "Outlet Hole" a quarter mile distant.

Later that morning, while patrolling the forested riverbank across the river from the boat ramp, I drove to high ground, a hidden place from which I could observe fishermen, both shore and boat anglers, at the Outlet Hole. At that time, there were 70 or so shore anglers along the banks and at least six boats in the 18-foot-deep hole that was roughly the area of two side-by-side football fields. I could see large king salmon breaking the surface here and there, but my attention was immediately drawn to the legless man in his big jet boat. He was up to no good. Every four or five seconds he would violently jerk upward on his rod, obviously attempting to snag salmon.

As I watched, I saw him hook into a big fish. His rod immediately bent hard over, and the fight was on. The struggle lasted nearly 15 minutes, near the end of which the exhausted fish was at times visible on the surface. The man grabbed a large landing net, and holding his rod high in his strong right arm, he wielded the net with his left arm, sliding it beneath the fish, which was coming in tail first. As he hefted the 18-pound fish aboard, I could see the hook on a large torpedo-shaped jig impaled in the underside of the fish, well behind its dorsal fin. The legless man immediately killed the fish with a wooden club and slipped it into a large ice chest.

He then pulled up the anchor. With biceps bulging, he brought it up, hand over hand, with no more trouble than any strong two-legged man. He now slid behind the controls, fired the engine and headed downstream toward the boat ramp. I drove the four miles around, crossed a bridge and arrived at the ramp in time to see him load the boat. After driving it onto the trailer, he hurried forward and lowered himself over the front of the boat onto the trailer's tongue. Balancing there on his stumps, he snapped the winch cable to the bow eyelet and winched the boat securely into place. Then, with his arms alone he hauled himself up and into the open pickup bed. From there he was a blur of motion as he scrambled forward and swung himself down and into the pickup's driver's seat without ever having touched the ground. I was amazed. His every move was so practiced, so polished. It was as though I had just watched a well-rehearsed circus act.

I contacted him then, driving down and parking near him on the ramp. When I walked to his window and identified myself, he seemed put out and a bit surly. Without asking him to exit the pickup, I asked to see his fishing and driver's licenses. He dug them out of his wallet, but he acted as though I was subjecting him to some unreasonable imposition.

"John David McHugh?" I asked, comparing his face to his DL photo.

"That's right," he said, "But people call me Shorty." With this, he pushed his door open and swung down to the ground. He stood there on his stumps, peering up at me, grinning at what he obviously considered a fine joke. I explained to him that I had watched him illegally snagging salmon and that I had observed him kill and retain a foul-hooked fish. His reaction was to simply shrug as if to say, "So what?"

I had decided before I contacted the man that because life had obviously dealt him an unfortunate hand, I would let him off with a warning. But early into my conversation with him, I was having second thoughts. He seemed totally remorseless and annoyed that I would disturb him over something so trivial as a salmon violation. But I explained to him the laws he had violated, and I informed him that I was letting him off that day with a warning. He reacted with indifference to what should have been welcome news. But he was genuinely annoyed when I explained that I would have to relieve him of the salmon I had watched him illegally catch. As I removed the large fish from his ice chest, I cautioned him against further violation of the fishing laws. He smiled, shaking his head as though he believed those laws somehow didn't apply to him. I drove away from him that day feeling resentful, dissatisfied with my decisions, convinced that I should have somehow handled things differently. But I was also certain that I had not seen the last of "Shorty" McHugh.

No more than a week later, McHugh was at it again, anchored in the Outlet Hole, doing his best to snag salmon. But this time he wasn't alone. A boy, about age 12, was with him and appeared to be having the time of his life. When McHugh illegally snagged into a salmon, he handed the rod to the boy whose grin was ear to ear as he struggled to reel in the big fish. It was an epic fight, but the boy finally prevailed. When McHugh netted the fish and hoisted it aboard, I clearly saw the jig hooked just behind the fish's dorsal fin.

I was again waiting at the boat ramp that afternoon, when McHugh and the boy returned. McHugh was not happy to see me. He declined my offer to help him load the boat, and again I was treated to a repeat performance of what I had witnessed the week before. Again, I was astonished at how totally capable he was, how effortlessly he got around in the boat and on the ground.

There was just one fish on the boat, and when I examined it I found deep hook wounds just behind the dorsal fin. The evidence I needed was there, but now I had to decide what to do with it. McHugh deserved to pay for his misdeeds, but I was very aware of how painful and difficult it would be to get a conviction on him. Did I really want to bring a man with no legs before a judge? And then there was a question of the boy. Did I really want to ruin what was probably one of the best days of his life? In the end, I chose to let McHugh off again, despite his continuing bad attitude, but not before getting him aside and delivering an up-close, low-volume, angry, teeth-clenched chewing-out that ended with me telling him that he would never get another warning from me. I then left them there and drove away, marveling in how soft I was becoming. I didn't even take the fish.

Due to the intensity of the warning I had growled into McHugh's ear, I expected him to retire from salmon poaching and take up a new hobby, but again I was wrong. Less than a month later, when I swung by the Outlet Hole, there was McHugh in his boat, fighting a salmon. I hadn't been there five minutes when he dragged the fish in tail-first, netted it and swung it into the boat. It was about a 15-pounder, and the jig's big hooks were impaled near its tail. McHugh, in a hurry for some reason, just dropped the netted fish onto the deck, pulled anchor, fired the engine and headed downstream for the boat ramp.

When I contacted him at the ramp, he already had his boat on the trailer, and I was astounded to see that the fish he had taken was still in the net on the deck where he had dropped it and the big hooks were still impaled near its tail. The illegal jig, in fact, was still attached to the line on his fishing outfit. I'd never before had evidence handed to me like that and I'd never seen such an utter lack of concern by a captured violator. True to my word, I issued McHugh a citation on that day. After photographing the still-hooked fish, still in the landing net, I seized into evidence the fish, the illegal jig and the fishing outfit and loaded it into my patrol rig. As I was writing the citation, McHugh shook his head, half-smiling and said, "You don't get it, do you? You'll never get a conviction on me. It just won't happen."

"Sign here, Mr. McHugh. I guess we'll find out." I then explained to him his court appearance date, gave him his copy of the citation and went on my way.

I was not surprised when I received a subpoena a few weeks later. McHugh had enlisted a public defender who had pled not guilty on his behalf and had requested a jury trial. I was there in front of the courthouse on the trial date and I was puzzled, for

McHugh was nowhere to be seen. Then, my attention was drawn to the parking lot where an elderly woman was pushing someone in a wheelchair, a man with no legs. As they drew nearer, I recognized Shorty McHugh, a legless man I was certain could play a respectable game of tennis. But on this day, his head was lolled over to one side, a vacant expression on his face, and he was drooling. I knew instantly my day would not end well.

Adding to my distress, a visiting judge would be presiding over the trial, a man I had never met and who knew nothing of my character. When he called the case, he asked the public defender if his client was present. The attorney simply pointed to the wheelchair and the pitiful-looking, legless, apparently helpless wreck of a human being it contained. The judge regarded McHugh briefly and asked with disbelief, "This is the defendant?" The attorney answered, "It is, your honor."

The judge then asked, "Is the arresting officer present?" I stood up and said, "I'm here, your honor." The judge regarded me as though I had been caught drowning puppies. "And you arrested this defendant for what?"

"For illegally snagging salmon, your honor. Could I offer a brief explanation?"

"That won't be necessary, officer," said the judge, "I have all the information I need. This case is dismissed."

As I turned and walked from the packed courtroom, every eye was upon me. I saw no friendly faces anywhere, just outraged citizens experiencing various levels of revulsion, loathing and disgust. One outspoken woman summed up the feelings of most everyone present, addressing me under her breath as I passed by. "You heartless bastard!"

***

AUTHOR'S NOTE:

Now and then, I feel compelled as a writer to pass on bits of wisdom I acquired during my long career as a warden, helpful tips to guide the more inexperienced among you through the many pitfalls of our challenging profession. It is therefore in the spirit of helpfulness that I offer you the following advice:

NEVER pinch a man with no legs.

ABOUT THE AUTHOR

Author Terry Hodges is a retired Fish and Game patrol lieutenant. For most of his 30-year career, he supervised the wardens in two Northern California counties. Unlike most warden supervisors, he was a field man, leading his wardens from the front, doing hard-core warden work until the day he retired. He was also a pilot and spent hundreds of hours flying single-engine planes, mostly at night, directing his wardens to violators he spotted from the air.

As a vastly experienced 30-year veteran game warden, Terry writes with a special understanding of his colorful and often dangerous profession. The stories compiled in his books are considered by many to be the best of their kind, and readers come away with a vivid picture of what the lives of game wardens and conservation officers are really like.

Terry has received national writing awards and was three times chosen Writer of the Year by the *Outdoor Writers Association of California* (OWAC). In addition to his seven books, he has been a regular contributor to the Department of Fish and Game's magazine, ***OUTDOOR CALIFORNIA***. He served four years in the U.S. Coast Guard and received his

Bachelor of Science degree from California State University at Sacramento.

In 2006, Terry was inducted into the *California Outdoor Hall of Fame.*

THE
WARDEN FORCE
SERIES

All titles available in print, eBook, and audiobook format.
Visit **WardenForce.com** for more info and previews.

NIGHT RIDER: SEASON 1

The Midnight Ride of Bonnie and Clyde: Wardens tangle with a murderous mother-and-son poaching team.

Night Rider: A California warden pursues highly dangerous night-poachers of wild pigs.

Decisions: Wardens off the coast of Southern California's Catalina Island risk their lives to save the crew of a sinking commercial squid-fishing boat.

A Second Second Chance: A California game warden ambushes outlaw catfish fishermen using baby swallows for bait.

The Collectors: California wardens take on a nest of Nazi-worshiping, weapons-collecting, deer poaching outlaws.

Nothin' Personal: California wardens track down a thief who steals the head and antlers of another hunter's buck.

Bottom Feeders: California wardens go after a band of white-trash, sturgeon-poaching hillbillies with attitudes.

An Outing with Team Taylor: A California game warden and his family, on a short vacation, team up to capture antelope, bear and steelhead poachers.

Rookie: A rookie California game warden gets his first taste of his hazardous new career.

Grand Trickery: A California warden employs a magnificent bluff to catch outlaws night-poaching deer.

Tough Luck on the Little Sur: California wardens pursue gaunch-hook steelhead poachers.

Serial Poacher: Wardens pursue a disturbing and dangerous lone-wolf deer poacher.

The Vision: A boy's fondest dream comes true.

GRIM WITNESS: SEASON 2

A Matter of Little Choice: Wardens hunt down an exceptionally large and highly dangerous wounded mountain lion.

The Meaning of Pursuit: Fleeing felons and a wild, white-knuckle ride for a reserve game warden.

Gambler's Luck: A big-rig load of alfalfa holds a surprise hidden in a chamber among the bales.

The Departure of Bully's Luck: A cruel bully gets what he deserves.

Pollard on the Rock: An alert clerk at a one-hour photo shop sends wardens in search of outlaw houndsmen.

Fools and Small Victories: A warden targets a particularly destructive brand of violator.

Renegades: Wardens target a destructive pair of elk poachers.

Bear Crazy: A warden investigates the poaching of an exceptionally huge bear, killed with a broadhead arrow at a garbage dump.

A Message Delivered: Wardens hunt down antler thieves.

Sting: Wardens close in on a band of abalone poachers.

Cave Man: California wardens tangle with a wild-looking, hairy, commercial crab fisherman from Oregon.

Skinny Bob: California wardens go undercover to capture commercial reptile rustlers.

Grim Witness: Dangerous pot-growing poachers use pipe bombs to kill king salmon.

Delta Ghosts: Season 3

Delta Ghosts: A team of wardens ambush outlaw gillnetters at Grizzly Bay, in the same Delta waters patrolled 80 years earlier by Fish Patrol warden and famous writer, Jack London.

Smooth Operator: Wardens stalk a cagy and arrogant abalone-poaching commercial sea urchin diver.

Time Bomb: A dangerous and mentally unstable deer poacher proves highly troubling for pursuing wardens.

Cheaters: An inexperienced warden consults an old pro of his profession to capture a pair of super-wary striped bass snaggers.

Tiger's Revenge: A cocky and confident salmon poacher makes the mistake of "pulling the tail of the tiger;" that is, taunting a local game warden.

A Calculated Risk: Despite a comedy of errors, wardens close in on highly destructive pig poachers.

Killer John: Future serial killer? Wardens deal with a scary deer poacher and born killer.

New Talent: A new warden astounds a mentor with his almost super-human sensory skills.

Slow Learners: A one-time major league pitcher proves to be a highly interesting adversary for wardens.

Davie Crockett and the Bush Baby: A Hollywood stunt man and elk poacher tangles with border wardens.

Then Came Speedy: A Peruvian sheepherder and a small sheepdog pay dearly to save their sheep from marauding bears in high meadows of the Sierra Nevada range.

Lethal Intent: Would-be assassins are thwarted by a fearless warden who puts his life on the line for the intended victims.

Cold, Cold Hearts: Season 4

Trash Can Joe: Wardens pursue an infamous, outlaw hunting-guide who uses donuts to illegally bait bears. Meet "The Black Robinhood."

Callous Hearts: A rogue band of meth-cooking deer poachers meets with misfortune.

Rascal's Road to Justice: "The world's greatest duck caller," as a renowned waterfowl violator bills himself, crows that he's too smart to be caught. His education to the contrary soon follows.

True Remorse: One of the coldest of the cold, cold hearts pays a heavy price for extreme cruelty to a trapped bear.

Turkeys: The wardens meet a hardened criminal whose hobbies are turkey hunting and home-invasion robberies.

A Weekend with "Starsky and Hutch": A swashbuckling pair of wardens cram a fourth-story, roof-to-roof foot chase in old San Francisco and heroic rescues from burning buildings into a single, memorable weekend.

The Natural: A young woman proves that she was born to be a Fish and Game warden.

Dirty Harry and Ape Island: A warden thinks his way out of a jam in this story that features a good-humored Highway Patrol sergeant and an ill-humored monkey.

Lucky Breaks: A warden demonstrates his substantial tracking skills to put away an outlaw houndsman who traffics in bear gallbladders.

Lobster Jake: An infamous lobster pirate teams with "The Muppet," a character straight out of a nightmare.

Cold, Cold Hearts: A California warden, at great risk to himself, flies to Alaska to help state troopers there deal with a team of highly dangerous, cruel and destructive grizzly poachers.

Delta Ambush: Season 5

Uncatchable 'Chick' Feathers: A clever deer-poaching archer, widely considered to be too smart to catch, meets an old-time game warden who disagrees.

Incident at Killer Cove: Armed killers on the run tangle with game wardens on the prowl.

Sooner or Later: An outlaw falconer outsmarts a new and inexperienced game warden. A year later, he's not so lucky.

Otter Killers and Uncommon Luck: Wardens pursue sea-otter-killing commercial abalone divers.

Leo's Demise: One man dies before wardens deal with an African lion, a grown pet gone rogue, in the suburbs of Los Angeles.

Tough Customers: A game warden and a hostage-taking armed robber nearly destroy a drugstore.

Bug Pirates: Trap-raiding lobster thieves meet with misfortune.

Setliners: Wardens target long-line catfish poachers.

A Matter of Preference: Wardens attempting to ambush season-jumping commercial lobster fishermen get a big surprise.

Delta Ambush: Night-prowling, canoe-borne wardens stalk a wily and destructive Delta outlaw.

Rake Man: A well disguised warden outsmarts lawless abalone pickers.

The Honest-to-God Truth: An honest mistake and a white-knuckle, midnight vehicle tail through Long Beach yields a surprise and an important arrest.

Raid of the Stockton Airborne: Did they or didn't they? Wardens from the sky? A day for mass-killing duck poachers does not end well.

Ordeal at Skull Canyon: Season 6

Scum of the Delta: A lone warden faces three armed and dangerous outlaws at night on a lonely Delta island.

Night of the Beach Walkers: Wardens set a trap for renegade abalone pickers on an island off the California coast.

The High Cost of Greed: A massive overlimit of snow geese equals bad news for greedy poachers.

The Best Medicine: A young boy provides a cure for racial tension.

Ordeal at Skull Canyon: A dark night and a mistake on an offshore island nearly proves fatal for a young warden.

Hoffman's Lucky Shot: A lucky break spares the evil life of a dangerous poacher.

Moseley's Reward: A well timed tip sets wardens on the trail of outlaw mountain lion trappers.

Herpie and the Snake Lady: Wardens raid an absolute house of horrors and target lawless reptile dealers.

Road Hunter: A road-hunting pheasant poacher leads a clever warden to pull off the most spectacular arrest of his career.

Harold's Toughest Race: A tough, marathon-running warden amazes everyone by running down an escaping would-be rapist.

Fatal Flaw: One dark mountain night, a lone warden, at great personal risk, bluffs a lawless band of brush-cutters to arrest a deer poacher and a wanted felon.

Tuffy's Sweet Moment: An epic foot chase ends in near death for a fleeing violator.

An Ending of Sorts: A warden-turned-writer, one winter's evening, reflects on his career and that of his long-dead mentor.

Deadly Intent: Season 7

Skin-Head Fred: Wardens tangle with a murderous, meth-cooking, game-killing Neo-Nazi.

Spreaders: Wardens target a highly intelligent, super-wary commercial lobster pirate.

Deadly Intent: An alert warden stays alive and saves a life.

The Poor Eyesight of Love: The arrest of a man and wife poaching team reminds wardens that love can indeed be blind.

Ruthless: Crossbow-wielding, night-hunting outlaws face sly wardens who never give up.

Ghost of the Feather: Salmon poachers on the Feather River mix it up with an old pro warden.

Abalone Boy: An abalone-poaching commercial sea urchin diver earns his way into state prison.

Anything but Cheap: A tough young warden targets ruthless, bear-killing houndsmen.

Knock-and-Talks: A highly experienced, slick-talking warden outsmarts goose and deer poachers.

Woody Peckerwood: A dumb crook story in which the dumb crook steals the wrong man's boots.

Kegger: Wardens break up a midnight keg party, and a gutsy college student becomes an instant legend.

The Troubling Case of Walter Sumpter: A highly troubled teenager commits a terrifying crime with ominous implications.

Masters of Destruction: Season 8

A Matter of Survival: A warden's worst fear nearly comes true.

Some Kind of No Good: A warden's exceptional skill and some blind luck combine for an interesting outcome.

Payback Time: The vengeful victim of a childhood bully retaliates years later, his revenge spectacular.

Drop-Countin' at Gunner's Swamp: A long-retired warden helps two employed wardens make an important duck overlimit case.

Threats and Promises: A search warrant search of the home of two deer poachers yields surprises, plus a brush with a bad cop.

An Extra Set of Eyes: An aging game warden lieutenant, a few days following knee surgery, ends up being far more than an observer during the action-packed, nighttime arrest of salmon poachers.

Operation High Hog: A large team of wardens pit their wits against some of the worst deer and pig poachers in California history.

Primal Instincts: Wardens pursue the puzzling case of two deer poachers who kill far more deer than they could ever use.

Combat Fishing: An old warden, his days of foot-chases far behind him, employs stealth and trickery to capture two fleet-footed young salmon poachers.

Masters of Destruction: A fearless and horribly destructive ATV-riding deer poacher repeatedly evades wardens and officers of other agencies before finally going down hard.

The Ghosts of Tipper Slough: A wealthy farmer pays far more than money when he ignores a warden and destroys a particularly wonderful wetland.

Leonard's Bad Word: Does a warden known for never using profanity have a slip-up over his radio one dark night?

Trophy Poacher: A disturbing, physically imposing, trophy-hunting poacher and a monster wildfire put wardens to the test.

www.ingramcontent.com/pod-product-compliance
Lightning Source LLC
Chambersburg PA
CBHW020254030426
42336CB00010B/763